Toad Triumphant

THE TALES OF THE WILLOWS

WILLIAM HORWOOD

Toad
Triumphant

Illustrated by Patrick Benson

HarperCollins*Publishers*

HarperCollins*Publishers*
77–85 Fulham Palace Road,
Hammersmith, London W6 8JB

Published by HarperCollins*Publishers* 1995
1 3 5 7 9 8 6 4 2

A catalogue record for this book
is available from the British Library

ISBN 0 00 225309 7

Set in Bembo

Printed in Great Britain by
HarperCollinsManufacturing Glasgow

Contents

· I ·

In Mr Toad's Garden

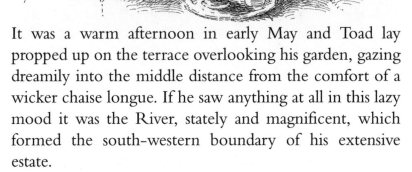

It was a warm afternoon in early May and Toad lay propped up on the terrace overlooking his garden, gazing dreamily into the middle distance from the comfort of a wicker chaise longue. If he saw anything at all in this lazy mood it was the River, stately and magnificent, which formed the south-western boundary of his extensive estate.

Toad had been employed thus all day, doing what he liked best, which was basking in past glories, contemplating present delights, and planning future triumphs.

Having spent the morning dwelling on his glorious past (as he saw it), he had risen up for sufficient time to take lunch and enumerate his many present pleasures while he did so. Now, well fed and watered, and supine once more, he had arrived at that stage in the day's work that required that he formulate plans for the coming months and years.

This was a moment Toad had been very much looking forward to, for he liked nothing better than thinking up schemes, preferably grand and clever ones that showed the world what a wonderful and extraordinary animal he was. He was by no means lacking in such ideas, and he was just getting into the swing of things with some preliminary thoughts of solo ascents of certain obscure Alpine peaks, when his peace was suddenly disturbed by the distant jangling of his front-door bell.

"I say," he called to his butler; "be sure to remember that I am not at home to *any*one for *any*thing!"

Toad had no wish to rise again till it was time for tea and he hoped very much that his new butler, already well instructed in such matters, would send the unwelcome visitor packing. As his man set off purposefully towards the front door, Toad felt the warming sun upon his face and, putting the caller out of his mind, returned to the contemplation of the future.

He was not short of schemes to contemplate, though he had no intention whatsoever of putting any of these plans into effect immediately. For one thing he did not have the means just then, having spent a great deal of money in the past year and a half rebuilding Toad Hall, which had been ruined by fire two years previously.

Generous as Lloyd's of London had been in its settlement of his insurance claims, for some reason it would not agree to provide Toad with funds to purchase all the medieval French tapestries, Mogul carpets, eighteenth-century English carved furniture and Wedgwood tea sets that a single gentleman such as he considered essential to the continuing comfort and entertainment of himself and his guests.

Not that Mr Toad was short of what people of less refinement than himself liked to call "a bob or two". No, he still had wealth enough to live a life of idle luxury, and intended to continue to do so to the end of his days, right up to the very last second, when he hoped he might still have a glass of bubbling Moet & Chandon in his right hand and a good Havana in his left as he passed into happy oblivion. Live now and don't pay later, that was Toad's motto. Nevertheless, the destruction of Toad Hall and its re-creation on more modern lines had served to remind him that even his resources were limited, and it was as well that he had been insured, for which precaution he had his late father to thank and not himself.

But in all truth, even if unlimited means had been there to support Toad's grandiose schemes and plans, the will and energy were not. He was not as young as he had been and was more cautious in taking risks with the outside world, which is to say the world beyond the River Bank.

Twice in recent times, once in consequence of unwittingly stealing a motor-car, and a second time as a result of an unfortunate accident in a flying machine that led to arraignments on dozens of charges, the most humiliating of which concerned a false allegation of dishonourable intentions regarding a chimney sweep's wife, Mr Toad had found himself awaiting trial in the dour dungeons of the Town's Castle.

If that was bad, the trials that followed, with their baffling procedures, mean-spirited cross-examinations, cold-hearted judges, and uncertain outcomes, were far worse, and Mr Toad wished never to suffer such trial and tribulation again. His generous and long-suffering friends, in particular the wise Badger, the practical Water Rat, and the inestimable Mole, had suggested that lest he forget — and they greatly feared that one day he might — it would be wise to have inscribed in stone the warning given to Toad by the High Judge at his last trial:

"Commit no more crimes, or all those sentences of execution eternal will be put back on the list from which they have not been fully expunged, and can never be, and we fear there will be no second chance."

A master mason duly carved these words in stone not once but thrice, and the chastened Toad was persuaded to erect these panels at places about his home where he might daily see them, namely above his bed, above his front door, and opposite his chair in the dining room. All agreed that this was but a small price to pay for Toad's continuing liberty.

After further thought the Badger had prudently seen to it that in addition to the three stone tablets, two large notices were painted, featuring the six key words of the High Judge's warning in large, black, accusing letters: "THERE WILL BE NO SECOND CHANCE!"

These had been placed facing *inwards* at the main entrance to Toad Hall and at the gate near the River, so that should he be tempted to lapse into his bad old ways and set off on some impetuous scheme he would see again the grim warning, and be persuaded to turn back onto the straight and narrow path once more.

These precautions had indeed made a deep impression on Toad, so much so that he was happy enough to formulate his plans through the course of that afternoon and then reject them one by one, for he had no desire to tumble into the dark void of criminality once more. Not that he was even then quite free from fear that the long arm of the law, and its unwelcome appendages the rough hands of the constabulary, might reach out and grasp him by the collar and drag him back into custody.

For which reason, when the jangling of the front-door bell suddenly ceased and he heard footsteps that were clearly not his butler's echoing towards him through the halls and chambers of Toad Hall, Toad sat up in alarm and began to wonder as the footsteps grew nearer still whether he should set in motion one of his escape plans.

He stood up and cast an eye down the length of his garden to the boat-house. Only two people knew what lay therein – he and his butler, one of whose first services had been to help Toad install by dead of night his secret means of escape: a powerful motor-launch, which lay under tarpaulins in the deeper recesses of the boat-house, primed and ready, its existence disguised by a punt and two skiffs. Toad had hoped he might never have to use the hidden launch,

11

and somewhat surprisingly had felt no thrill at all when he had first seen it.

"I shall not touch this craft!" he had cried out to the baffled gentleman who had guided it down-river to Toad Hall, already much surprised that a most strict condition of the sale included nocturnal and silent delivery. He was the more surprised because such a launch as this, of high quality and great expense, was normally used by explorers to unknown and dangerous parts, such as the upper reaches of the Amazon, or the crocodile-infested swamps of New Guinea, rather than the quiet and placid middle reaches of the River.

"Machines," continued his eccentric client, "are no more for me! They have caused me too much misery in the past, and my friends too much trouble. The day, or night, I have need to use this powerful craft as a means of escape is that last day I shall be here at the Hall, and happy."

"You will not be taking it out for pleasure purposes then, sir? It is to stay under wraps, unused and unenjoyed?"

"Indeed," declared Toad. "For many years, I hope. But, alas, lesser and ordinary people such as yourself, or my butler here, do not quite understand that great personages such as myself make many enemies and must be prepared for the worst. Unjust accusers may seek me out, my enemies may desire to return me to gaol and unfair trial, and if they do only then shall I leap into this launch and embark upon the life of a fluvial fugitive!"

Toad meant it, every word. His days of tangling with the law were over and he was reformed, the secret craft to be used only in the event of past chickens coming home to roost.

It was with these thoughts uppermost, and now poised for flight, that he heard the footsteps cease, watched as the door to the garden opened and was relieved to see not ten arresting officers, but his good friend the harmless Mole.

"Toad!" said the Mole, coming forward at once. "Your butler suggested that you might not be pleased to see me, but when I explained –"

Toad was very pleased to see him, very pleased indeed, not so much because of who he was, but because of who he was not.

"My dear chap!" cried Toad, hopping about from one foot to another with relief and mopping his brow. "I *am* happy to see you, even though I am feeling frail and weak after a hard morning's work and ought not to receive guests. But –"

"I have come to ask your advice, Toad."

Toad ceased speaking, but did not immediately close his mouth, so startled was he by the Mole's words.

"Your advice, Toad: I need it," repeated the Mole persistently, thinking perhaps that his friend had suddenly been taken ill. Not only was his mouth agape, but his eyes had taken on a glazed and bulging look.

"Advice?" he gasped, trying to remember a single occasion when anyone had asked for his advice. For his money, yes. His time, that too. Various of his possessions, certainly. But his advice? Never.

It did not take Toad long to recover from the shock, however.

"My dear Mole," he said robustly, "there are certainly many things I might advise you on, for you are but a modest fellow with a very limited experience of life who is no doubt uncertain of himself in many ways. Whereas I, Toad of Toad Hall, naturally have a very great deal of good advice which I am ready and willing to offer on most subjects.

"But before you inform me of the matter that concerns you, pray sit down. Make yourself comfortable while I lie down again, for my back aches a little and I must rest —"

"Shall I fetch tea for your guest and yourself, sir?" offered the butler, grasping the first opportunity he could to interrupt his master's torrent of words.

"Tea? Of course, fetch tea," said Toad cheerfully. "A capital idea, eh Mole? But let our tea be accompanied by something more fortifying, for Mr Mole looks as if he needs it. Champagne, I think."

"No, really, Toad; not so early in the day!" said the Mole as the butler set off about his work.

"Nonsense, Mole, you need a little comfort in your life. My first piece of advice to you is to enjoy life more, and to move from those miserable quarters of yours at Mole End and –"

"But I like my home," said the Mole quietly, looking uneasily about the many windows, doors, embayments and wings of Toad's great place. "It takes little looking after and provides me with everything I need."

"Each to his own, I suppose; but what other advice can I offer you?"

·"Well, I – I was hoping – I was thinking that per- haps –" began the Mole, clearly very much concerned by something he found hard to address.

"You have had my advice on the matter of your gen- eral comfort," interrupted Toad, not really wanting to listen at all and preferring the sound of his own voice to that of Mole's; "now perhaps I may add to that with some advice concerning your friends."

"My friends?" repeated the Mole, much surprised.

Such friends as he had – and he counted Toad among them – were very long established and he could not imagine how Toad might "add" anything to the subject. Yet the Mole knew Toad very well, very well indeed, and he had half expected some such interview as this, in which Toad would do most of the talking and he most of the listening. But then again, the Mole had nowhere else to turn for advice and counsel upon the particular matter that worried him, and perhaps if he sat patiently for long enough Toad would run out of steam.

For Mole was worried, very worried indeed. So much so that as Toad began to launch forth on the subject of friends the Mole felt the same inexplicable malaise that had afflicted him for some weeks past come over him again, and though the afternoon was the finest yet that year, and tea was on its way, and Toad for all his faults had welcomed him and was striving to make him feel comfortable and at ease – despite all that, the Mole felt tears well up; and not for the first time in the past few days.

"O dear! O dear!" he muttered to himself, rising up to advance past Toad to the edge of the terrace to view the estate, so that Toad could not see him make a fool of himself. "O my! O my!"

Oblivious as always, Toad carried on talking behind him, on and on, for which the Mole was grateful, for he felt his normal stability and calmness begin to return.

"Eh, Mole? And what do you say to that?" concluded Toad, thinking that the Mole had heard and understood every word.

The Mole dabbed at his eyes and sniffed a little to regain his composure. "I'm sorry, Toad, I was admiring the view and missed the last part of what you said."

"I was saying, Mole, I was suggesting, in fact I was *advising* that you should widen your acquaintance beyond that very limited circle which I believe it presently comprises, namely Ratty, Badger and Otter."

"There is also my Nephew," said the Mole rather feebly, feeling that he was very lucky to have such good friends and kin as these, very lucky indeed, and he had no need of more: "They are really very good to me."

"Good to you! Pooh! You are good to *them*! I have nothing against Ratty or Badger, of course I do not, and as for your Nephew I dare say he has been of some service to you –"

"And to you as well, Toad, I believe –" the Mole could

not help adding, for he knew well that Nephew had been of great help to Toad in the rebuilding of the Hall, successfully representing him on delicate matters with such people as builders and architects where one or other of the parties affected had been upset and affronted; matters in which Toad was quite incapable of representing himself without compounding matters for the worse.

"Yes, your Nephew has certainly benefited from my tutelage, Mole, and I'm gratified that you mention it, for I may say that I am not so immodest as to do so myself. I believe, too, he has acted on my advice from time to time, which is no doubt why you have come here today to ask for my help and counsel?"

"Er, yes —" began the Mole, not quite happy to put such a construction on matters, but willing enough to concede the point if it meant he was offered the listening ear he so desperately needed.

"Well then," said Toad at last, "and what is it that's troubling you?"

"Well —" essayed the Mole, "there *has* been something that has worried me lately, worried me very much, and I am most grateful that you are willing to listen to me, for it may really seem rather inconsequential to one such as yourself, but to me —"

It was unfortunate, most unfortunate in the event, that it was just at this moment, which it had taken the Mole so long to reach (for his planned interview with Toad had been many days in the making, and it had required a good deal of courage on his part to make the trek from Mole End to Toad Hall and ring the bell), that the butler returned with tea.

His arrival put a stop to further conversation, for there are few things in the world more certain to remind gentle-folk of the fact that if all is not well now it very soon will be, than the sight of a well-trained English butler emerging onto the sunny garden terrace of a gentleman's residence, bearing a brass-handled tray bedecked with the many items that make for a successful open-air tea.

Such items, if properly prepared and portered, jingle and tinkle, twinkle and shine, as if to announce their approach, and all the cups and saucers, the silver spoons and the sugar bowl, the steaming hot water and the shin-ing strainer, the teapot and the plate of delicate sand-wiches — all seem to combine and say as one, "Let your worries cease for now; the world is aright again!" And in the welcome pouring of the tea and the delightful crunch of the cucumber and cress sandwiches, not to mention the promise of the coming cakes and the possible surprise of strawberries and cream to follow, all else is held at bay: the past is forgotten, the future does not exist, and all is peace.

Such was the effect of the arrival of tea upon Toad and Mole. Toad ceased his prattle while Mole put aside his still unspoken difficulties, and both tucked in.

When talk resumed, it was about inconsequential things such as Mr Toad's new butler, by whom the Mole was much impressed.

"I am glad you think so, Mole, for you are certainly right. Prendergast is one of the finest butlers in all the land and has turned down offers of employment from Earls, Dukes and possibly Kings so that he may serve me. Such are the perquisites deriving from the fame and

general respect that Toad of Toad Hall is able to command —"

For this was indeed that same Prendergast who had once been in the employ of no less a personage than the High Judge himself in his great residence east of the Town, in whose welcome confines Toad had once been a fraudulent guest. On that occasion, some two years earlier, which had to do with a trifling matter of a flying machine and a glass-shattering descent by parachute into His Lordship's hothouse, a curious bond of affection and friendship had grown up between Toad and His Lordship's butler (now former butler) Prendergast.

Nobody, in society or out of it, had been more surprised and delighted than Toad when his advertisement in *The Times* for a manservant had attracted a reply from his old friend — as he thought of him. He naturally, but wrongly, assumed that Prendergast had applied for the post out of respect and the honourable prospect of serving a gentleman as noble, and as famous, as himself. But this was not quite the case.

The plain fact was that Prendergast had come into a small inheritance from a relative in Australia and though he had no desire to be idle and unemployed, his zest for serving Lords and Ladies of the genuine kind had waned after a quarter of a century in their service at the highest levels. Now he could pick and choose, and, examining the columns under "Manservants" in that august organ one day, he had been astonished and delighted to see that there was a vacancy at Toad Hall.

Prendergast had many qualities, not all of them quite as conservative as the greatest of butlers generally aspire to.

In this respect the qualities that Toad's advertisement had excited were those of adventure, change, and good humour. He had never forgotten Toad's arrival at His Lordship's residence, nor the pleasures that came with serving one who was without doubt more vain and self-centred than any he had served before – and one who did that which Lords and Ladies too rarely did: bravely made a fool of himself and, shrugging off one disaster, promptly created another.

After so many years of sober, dull and unamusing service of the highest rectitude Prendergast had decided that before emigrating forever to Australia he wished to serve – and to serve to the very best of his ability – a master as reprehensible and notorious as Mr Toad of Toad Hall.

He had desired the post so much that he had felt quite nervous in making his application for it, and had greatly feared that Mr Toad would either not remember him, or would not be willing to have in his employ one who had served that same High Judge before whom Toad had been tried. He was also concerned that he might feel embarrassed to interview for such a post someone who had on two occasions tipped him a shilling – once when Toad had escaped from His Lordship's House in the guise of a sweep, and then when Toad had been escorted by his gaoler to the edge of the Town after his trial and warned never to return.

He quite underestimated Toad, who not only remembered him, but remembered him most happily, and was overjoyed to secure such a catch. Their mutual feelings were therefore ones of admiration and even affectionate memory, like two doughty campaigners who, having been through one war together, find themselves thrown together by Fate for another.

Prendergast's first duty on arrival – almost before he had removed his coat – had been to assist in the night-time delivery of Toad's powerful new motor-launch and to secrete it within the boat-house. This was not the kind of duty that normally comes an English butler's way by night *or* day, and Prendergast there and then decided that his confidence in Toad was well placed indeed. In all of England's wide and pleasant land, in all the Empire per-haps, no butler went about his work so happily as Prendergast, and none relished more the challenge of the months ahead. For months only Prendergast had decided it would be, and had told his new employer as much.

"I am, sir, of course much honoured that you feel I am suitable for this post, but I must give you notice now that I can only accept the position for six months. I have pressing business in the Antipodes and propose to set sail in October at the latest."

"My dear fellow," said Toad heartily at this interview, and with that inappropriate familiarity which he carried off so well, "six months will see us on our feet at the rebuilt Toad Hall. Train up the staff in that time and see that my worries and cares are seen to and I shall be well pleased."

"It is agreed then, sir," said Prendergast respectfully.

The Mole found all this most interesting, but he was now tired and defeated, for from the moment tea had arrived he had been forced to give up all further attempts at seeking Toad's advice. The story of Prendergast done, all Toad wanted to talk about was the awfulness of having so much money, and the stress and strain of rebuilding Toad Hall and having to cope with an obstructive architect (as it seemed to Toad) and an obtuse and unintelligent clerk of works (as Toad saw it). Meanwhile the Mole, who had heard it all before, could not but notice how warm and soporific the sun felt on his face, how much better he felt for the tea he had just had, how buzzingly the bees seemed to buzz and tunefully the birds to sing – in short, how pleasant things seemed to have become and how unimportant his own little concerns suddenly seemed . . .

"Mole! Mole!"

Toad's imperious cry awoke the Mole from the blissful sleep into which he had drifted. Evidently he had said all he wanted to about architects, clerks of works, and the difficulty of being the patron of so large a project as the rebuilding of Toad Hall, and now wished to draw the Mole's attention to something else.

"Well, Mole, and what do you say to this?"

The tea things had gone and so had the butler, and the sun had begun to settle a little. Toad held aloft a very large sheet of drawing paper upon which the Mole could see many lines and squiggles, and a good deal of writing. Mole saw that it was a plan to rebuild the garden, and a very clear and thorough one too.

"Yes, but do you see what is written there, Mole?" moaned Toad. "O, my head throbs and my body aches with the effort of thinking of it all. Can you not help me come to some decision?"

Mole rubbed his sleepy eyes and tried to focus on where Toad pointed, which was a small area on the plan in which nothing appeared to have been drawn or written at all, and around which a thin black line had been described. No flower beds there it seemed, no trees or walls or fountains. Nothing at all.

Mole read aloud the words that seemed to have given Toad such trouble: "*Client to decide*".

"Decide what?" asked the Mole.

"That's just it. Something has to go there but the landscape architect, brilliant as he is, was unable to decide and has turned to me for help and advice."

"Might it not be that he just wishes you to have a say in the design of at least one small area of your garden?"

"No," said Toad peremptorily, dismissing this reasonable and accurate conclusion, "that's not it at all, Mole. No, he knows he has failed at the final hurdle and looks to me for guidance and decisive help!"

"It seems," said the Mole, "that a good deal of the preliminary work has already been done, and already some of the plantings made."

The Mole looked at the garden once more, this time with some regret. Gone were the ancient fish ponds and the pigeon house of former times; gone the scented rose beds and the arboured ways where once Toad and his River Bank companions had strolled, he talking in his vain and conceited way, they indulging him. Yet nostalgic though Mole felt, he could not but reflect that it was typical of Toad, and a quality that the Mole rather admired, that it was not the sentimental embrace of the old that held him back, as it held back so many others, but the beckoning of the new that called him forward.

While Toad wrestled with that small area left for him to decide, the Mole tried to imagine the garden as it would one day be and with the plan before him it was not, after all, so difficult. How magnificent and well grown those herbaceous borders would be, with an avenue of limes and a pergolaed walk overhung with honeysuckle and vines, a fountain sparkling in the sun, a sunken garden, a rose bed, two vast and impressive herbaceous borders filled with plants at the peak of their bloom, and down by the River some fresh new willows.

Quite suddenly the Mole spoke up, saying, "How much I would like to be here to see this garden grown to its full glory once more, how very much. I do admire you, Toad, for your foresight in planning such a thing for future generations."

He said these words with gentleness and sincerity, and if there was a moistness in his eyes now it was not for the matter that had so troubled him when he had first come, but rather out of mild regret that while he had his

Nephew as a link to future generations, among all their friends along the River Bank, only the Otter had offspring to take things forward. The wayward Portly might still be somewhat unreliable, but soon enough he would grow up to be something more than he now was: the young so often finally surprise the old. He or his young would see this garden grow.

But for the rest of them, mused the Mole, there was nobody to whom to pass fond memory, or bequeath future hope, and when they were gone they would be all gone, and this grand plan of Toad's – perhaps the grandest and the best and the most useful he had caused to be made – would be seen by none that were their kin.

"O my!" whispered the Mole, as much to himself as Toad. "How strangely my thoughts ebb and flow these days, and how much more I seem to see than there really is – perhaps, after all, that is my difficulty and the cause of my distress."

Then his eyes moistened once more, but now the Mole discovered that just as *he* had not been listening to Toad before, now Toad was not listening to him. Instead he was staring fixedly at that vacant plot on the terrace about which he had to decide.

"There it was all the time and I couldn't see it!" said Toad in a strange low voice, alarming in its intensity. "How clever I am, but what of that? Genius is not too bold a word. How sensible of this landscape architect to entrust *me* with the only important decision of the whole design!"

The Mole had seen his friend in many moods, but he had never seen him quite like this. He watched in astonishment and some disquiet as an extraordinary change came over Toad's face. His normal look of vanity and conceit mixed with cowardice, self-concern and personal indulgence was slowly supplanted by a look of all-consuming triumph, much as a rising sun consumes the trivial shadows of dawn. This was Toad in alarming transmutation.

Accompanying this change was another in Toad's stance, which till then had been somewhat hunched and intense. Now Toad began to straighten and to raise himself up into a pose that seemed to suggest that the terrace was too small for him, and that it would not be very long before the whole garden was too small as well.

"Why, Toad," said the Mole quietly, "what is it that you see?"

Toad turned slowly to him – the Mole could have sworn that he stared down at him as a god might stare down from Mount Olympus – and he said in a strange and distant way, "I have seen the way to immortality."

"Immortality?" stuttered the Mole.

"Yes, immortality," said Toad. "Now, Mole, leave me, for I have important arrangements and preparations to make."

"O dear!" said Mole, for he saw that an unwelcome and all too familiar wildness had returned to Toad's eyes, a kind of madness, the pursuit of which would surely lead him astray as it had so often done in the past.

"Immortality has beckoned and I must respond," said Toad grandly, "even if it means I must leave my friends behind. I hope that at some future time, in some future place we shall meet again."

"In some future time and place?" echoed the Mole, now very considerably alarmed. "Are you feeling quite well, Toad? Are you expecting something dire to happen about which you might like to speak?" The Mole had a notion that Toad had seen the spectre of the Grim Reaper, scythe and all, already stalking along the River Bank in their direction, and the Mole did not like it. It betokened delusions of grandeur and excesses of behaviour which so many of Toad's friends had feared would one day return and finally destroy him.

"Please, Toad," said the Mole, "won't you lie down, for perhaps the sun has gone to your –"

"Leave now," said Toad in an unnatural, other-worldly way. "Leave me now!"

Such was his gesture of dismissal then – not unkind exactly, but certainly absolute and forbidding – that the Mole could not but obey it. In any case it was quite plain to Mole that this was a matter about which the Badger needed to be informed, and urgently. So the Mole did as Toad bade him, and hurried off down through the garden towards the exit onto the River Bank, alarmed for Toad and somewhat miserable for himself.

As he reached the gate the Mole turned and looked back up towards the Hall, a sense of fateful foreboding coming over him. What he saw only served to increase it.

For Toad had moved to that vacant plot that he had been asked to decide about. He now stood within it, his hands and arms raised towards the early evening sky, one leg extended a little behind him and the other doing its best to sustain his weight. The whole effect was emphasized and highlighted by the last rays of a setting sun.

What Toad was doing was a mystery to the Mole, but what he was hoping to achieve thereby was all too plain: he was seeking immortality, and it could lead to no good, no good at all.

Whispering "O dear!" to himself several times, and intent upon alerting his friends to the danger, the Mole turned away once more, and passed through the gate from Toad's estate out onto the River Bank.

In doing so he had to pass under the notice that the Badger had caused to be erected for the benefit of Toad against the day – distant as it seemed then, all too imminent as it seemed now – when he might again discover some new and dangerous idea and wilfully set off after it without a thought for the consequences to himself, or those along the River Bank: THERE WILL BE NO SECOND CHANCE!

·II·

Mole in the Doldrums

It had been Mole's firm intention after his frustrating interview with Toad to forget his own worries and go straight to the Badger to express his concern about their mutual friend's sudden lapse into behaviour that seemed likely to take him back into his bad old ways.

But deep and abiding though the Mole's sense of concern and responsibility for others was, on this occasion his own concerns got the better of him. He reached the bridge, beyond which the path to the Badger's home lay, but went no further. He paused for a time, stared down into the mysterious depths of the River, and that wistful and disquieting mood that had first led him to Toad's overtook him once more.

He turned back and made his lonely and unhappy way to Mole End. There, refusing all conversation with his Nephew, he sought comfort in sleep.

Before long it was the Mole rather than Toad who had become a cause of concern along the River Bank, for it was plain he had not been his normal cheerful self for many weeks past. His Nephew knew it, the Water Rat knew it, everyone along the River Bank knew it: why, even *he* seemed to know it. But none of them, not even the Mole himself, seemed to know quite why.

His Nephew had no explanation, and none of the Mole's friends seemed able to help. The Water Rat, for example, could make no sense of it at all and grew quite irritable and impatient as the Mole's gloominess and lack of interest in life continued, while Toad had time only for his own grand plans.

But Nephew did not give up easily, especially where the welfare of the Mole was concerned. No one in all the world meant more to him and he would leave no stone unturned, no course of action untried, in his efforts to help the Mole back to normality. So he decided to take his courage in his hands and call upon Mr Badger. The wisest of animals, the Badger had lived there longer than any of them, remembering a past none of them had ever known. Indeed, he was the only remaining animal living who could remember Toad's father.

Nephew had visited the Badger a good few times

alone, yet he always felt a sense of awe as he approached his house. It was not only that the Badger's moods were unpredictable – on occasion he chose not to answer the door at all – but also the sense of darkness and danger that the Wild Wood inspired in the hearts of those who did not live there. Even in broad daylight on a summer's day the place seemed dark, the trees huge, and what gaps there were between the trees filled with sinister, shifting shadows; while the rustling thickets, near and far, seemed to creak and groan with ill intent.

So when he had made his way to the centre of the Wild Wood that day and had finally built up the courage to knock at the Badger's door, he listened to the sound of movement inside, and then the bolts and chains being drawn and undone, with considerable relief.

Any fears regarding the Badger's response were soon dispelled, for he held the Mole in particular affection, and when Nephew explained the seriousness of the situation and his concern that no one had been able to help, the Badger needed little urging to forgo all else and depart for Mole End immediately, leading Nephew by the secret ways of the Wild Wood in silence, deep in contemplation.

When they arrived at Mole End, the Mole, ever courteous, served tea, and it was some time before the Badger felt he could get to the point.

"That fact is, Mole, that I've come to see you because I understand you are somewhat down in the dumps, and it's no good denying the fact. I thought you might care to unburden yourself to me?"

"O, I know you mean it for the best, Badger, and believe me I am greatly honoured that you have made this call on me, but I assure you there is nothing wrong," responded the Mole.

"Nothing at all?" queried the Badger, rather stumped by the Mole's calm denials.

"Nothing, really nothing," averred the Mole before adding, to change the subject, "now, please, have another cup of tea. Nephew, put that kettle on again and bring out that extra plate of cucumber sandwiches I prepared earlier —"

The Badger sighed, seeing that for now he could do nothing more. Though the Mole was putting on a brave face, the Badger could see the truth in his eyes: a definite gloominess and even, he told himself unhappily, a certain despair.

In the days that followed this well-meaning attempt to get to the bottom of the Mole's problem he seemed to decline yet further and nothing anyone could say or do made any difference.

A few nights later, when Nephew was away fulfilling a kindness for Toad, the Mole took a nocturnal walk. By what starry tear-stained routes he wandered that night none will ever know. The alarm would certainly have been raised by Nephew had he been at Mole End, but, fatally, he was not. So no one witnessed the Mole's distracted wanderings along the River and in the Wild Wood, over the rough ground of the open fields and along the uncut hedgerows in the black shadows of deepest night; no one saw his wild gaze searching the shifting stars and moon as he grew ever more tired and cold, unable to put a name to the despair he felt.

Perhaps he paused along the way to rest his weary head and aching limbs, hoping still to find an answer to that which worried him. None can tell. However it was, and however he got there, dawn found him sitting upon the obscure and reedy bank west of the island, that mysterious eyot that lies just a little way above the dangerous weir, whose threatening roar can be heard so plainly from that dark spot.

There sat the Mole, disconsolate among the reeds, his feet dangling in a back-eddy of water, his eyes gazing with fatal fascination upon the faster-flowing current a few yards out. This was no place for a land animal to be, nor was it one where even a strong swimmer, such as the Otter, or the Water Rat, would lightly go and sit, wetting his feet as the Mole now did.

There, alone and miserable, with the other inhabitants of the River Bank unaware of the crisis, the Mole slumped among the swaying reeds, drifting dangerously between sleep and wakefulness. By the time morning came, it was not just the Mole's feet that were in the water, but much of the lower half of his body, such that a watching animal might have thought that he was about to slip in the water for a swim – a very foolhardy swim, and one that might easily prove rather more final than most swims are meant to be.

Yet the Mole was not entirely alone and unobserved.

"'Ere! What's 'is game then?" hissed a common and vulgar voice among the shadows of the vegetation a little higher up the bank from the Mole.

The question was answered by a creature whose voice was no less insinuating and sibilant.

"That's Mr Mole of Mole End, if my eyes don't deceive me, and 'e's asking for trouble."

They were two stoats, those heartless and treacherous animals that inhabit the Wild Wood, out on a day's hunt for mischief and opportunity.

"Funny place to take a dip," said the first laconically.

"That won't be a dip, chum, that'll be a plunge."

"Let's watch and see what 'appens."

There was a period of silence as the Mole slipped perceptibly further into the water.

"Pound to a penny 'e won't surface more than once if 'e goes over the weir."

"Yer jokin'. 'E'll not get that far alive –"

And so did those wretched animals make mock of the Mole's misery, and make wagers upon its outcome.

It was not kindness that made them finally desist and hurry off to inform Mr Badger of the Mole's plight, but pecuniary advantage. They hoped that the Badger might reward them for their trouble, perhaps five pounds sterling or so.

"Five pounds. That's about the worth of Mole to

Badger and all those other animals, I reckon."

The Badger immediately set off to where the Mole was, by now nearly submerged, and having dragged his friend from the water, with more hindrance than help from the stoats, he came to certain conclusions about the affair, and made certain decisions, the most important of which was that the matter must not be talked about by any of them to anyone.

"If a word of this *private* business gets abroad," warned the Badger, "there will not only be no question of five pounds, five shillings or five pence, but the small matter of me pursuing the animal who talks of it and driving him from the River Bank forever! Is that clearly understood?"

"Yes, sir, Mr Badger, sir. You can rely on us; mum is certainly the word where we're concerned!" whined the cowardly stoats, who sang a very different tune with Mr Badger than they had while watching the defenceless Mr Mole.

"Let it be so!" said the Badger darkly as the stoats scampered off.

He turned his attention back to his friend the Mole, insisting that he should come back to the Wild Wood, and there be cared for in his rough but comfortable home, where perhaps the truth of what had happened might come out.

"No, really, I'm p-p-perfectly all right," the Mole insisted, his teeth chattering now with shock as well as cold as the Badger took off his waistcoat and draped it round him.

"No you're not, Mole," said the Badger firmly, "and

my home is a good deal nearer than your own. Now you come with me."

"But really, B–B–Badger I – I –"

How frail he seemed then to the Badger, and how close to tears.

"Come on, old fellow, you lean on my arm and I'll have you by a warm fire with your feet up in no time at all!"

"Well, I – p-perhaps it's for the b-best," said the Mole. "I do feel very tired, I really d-d-do."

The Badger put a reassuring arm about him and only then did the poor Mole finally sigh and lower his head, and sob out for the misery that had been so long in finding its expression.

"Come on, old chap," said the Badger thickly, for he was much moved by the Mole's open tears. "Come back and tell me what it is that troubles you."

The Badger put the Mole in a small but comfortable spare room, and here the Mole slept non-stop for two whole days after his ordeal. Then he began to emerge into a more waking state, to sit up in bed, and to take in the details of the Badger's spare room – a room he had never seen before, or even knew existed.

It was full of old mementoes and reminders of relatives no River-banker knew that the Badger had, and of pictures of places to which no animal thereabouts could ever have guessed the Badger had ever been. But there were other even more intriguing objects, the significance of which was unclear to the Mole. A few items of clothing hanging from a peg, clothes that seemed rather too small-for the Badger to wear now and which, he supposed,

must have been articles he wore when young. Altogether more mysterious was the calendar that hung above the bed, many years out of date, being of a year somewhat prior to the Mole's own arrival at the River Bank. Certain days in July and August of the year concerned were circled, and on the last day of September, in a hand that was certainly the Badger's own, these cryptic words were scribed: "*The Final Date*".

The Mole was touched, and his heart warmed, by the sight of a little row of youthful books, tatty and dusty now, which the Badger had preserved upon a shelf, and which bespoke an animal who had been brought up to read and study, and enjoy that love of learning that no doubt contributed to the good-hearted wisdom for which he was now so revered and loved.

It must be said, however (the Mole's curiosity having slightly got the better of him), that when he examined the books more closely he was surprised to see that they were mischievously scored and crayoned inside, and some of the illustrations had very juvenile emendations – such as spectacles on characters that surely wore none, and a crudely drawn crocodile about to attack some harmless ducks in a village pond – that suggested that the Badger had not always been quite so careful or reverential of his books as he was now.

The Mole would have liked to ask the Badger about the items he had seen when that kindly animal looked in from time to time with cups of tea and nourishing broth, but he felt it discreet and proper not to do so.

By the fourth day the Mole was well on the way to recovery, well enough to leave his bed – with some reluctance – and the Badger persuaded him to take a walk through the Wild Wood. How slowly he went, how miserably, and all the more so when they approached the River and he espied the willows in full green leaf beyond, and the landscape he knew and loved so well.

"Badger –" began the Mole.

"Yes?" said the Badger gently.

"It's nothing, nothing at all."

They walked on slowly till they reached a tree stump where the path from the Wild Wood meets the River.

"You look a little tired; I have let you come too far. Why not sit awhile before I take you back to my home? I shall go on and stand on the bank, for I like to view the River from this point, downstream and upstream –"

"Upstream," mumbled the Mole, "yes – I –"

The Badger let him sit down and went on the few more paces to the bank, much exercised about what he should do next. It was plain enough that the Mole was still most unhappy, but he had not yielded to the Badger's discreet enquiries, and he knew that he must be allowed to take his own time.

A little sob behind him: from the Mole. A little cry. The Badger could bear it no longer and turned to see a sight as pathetic and as moving as any he had ever seen. It was his good friend the Mole, sitting now on the stump, but hunched forward, trying his very best not to embarrass another with his emotions, but quite unable to stem the tide a moment longer.

"Why, Mole," began the Badger, going to him at once, "whatever is it? What can it possibly be that continues to distress you so? Can you not try to tell me at last?"

For a brief moment the Mole looked up at him, still trying to hold back the tears, till words began to tumble out at last and he wept, and wept.

"It didn't seem so much when – when I first suggested it – I didn't think it *mattered* – but – but –" The Mole wept some more before he was able to continue, and the Badger said not a word. "But, well, I put it to Ratty and he agreed and my hopes – my hopes went up – because, of course, you know, I could not do it myself, not *by* myself. I really have not much courage – he has the knowledge and the skill so I was relying on him and he agreed, he *did* agree, but then he said – he told me – he would not – O dear, Badger, I just do not have the courage to do it all alone. I was *relying* on him to help and, and –"

"You have a great deal of courage, Mole," said the Badger, daring to speak at last.

"Not for such a thing, not without Ratty; and then suddenly he – he said he could not – O, bother!"

Thus had the Mole begun to talk down by the River, and the Badger had led him home, let him sleep through the afternoon and when he had awoken feeling very much recovered, had given him a good supper. Then, even though it was early summer, he had lit a fire and the Mole had finally been persuaded to settle down and say what ailed him; and the more the Badger heard, the more he kicked himself for not understanding sooner.

"You see," began the Mole, "when spring came this

year a most strange desire to journey forth overcame me, a kind of restlessness to go up-river.

"It has been a long-held ambition of Ratty and myself to mount such an expedition and we have often talked of it during our picnics, but neither of us had ever felt inclined to take it further – till this spring.

"I was aware, of course, because Ratty told me so, that you have always strongly advised against such ventures, but so strong was the compulsion I felt for the expedition, and so persuasive my words to Ratty, that he agreed to lend his boat if I would provide the victuals. What is more, and here, Badger, I confess I feel some remorse, we decided to keep the matter secret from you, lest you endeavour to dissuade us from the enterprise."

The Badger growled somewhat ambiguously, and the Mole felt it wisest to hurry on with his story.

"Well then, rather to my surprise, Ratty was very easily persuaded to be party to my plan, and to take upon himself the practical side of the organization.

"Once the matter was agreed I found that an altogether new and unfamiliar sense of excitement overtook me. What had seemed a mere dream, a moment's fancy, had become solid certainty, and my mind began to dwell on what I might find upstream, which is to say – what I might find – *Beyond*."

"Beyond," murmured the Badger.

"But then suddenly everything changed. With the coming of Mayday everything turned warm and good and Ratty suddenly found much to do along the River Bank. He came to me and said, 'Perhaps we are rather over-reaching ourselves with this jaunt of ours. It's not that I do not want to go, Mole, old chap – and I would not want to disappoint you – but you must understand that the River Bank only stays as safe and peaceable as it does because I look after it so well, with Otter's help of course. Now there's so much to do –'

"Well, Badger, you know that I am not one to push myself forward, and if Ratty felt that he had better things to do than set off on a mere jaunt, well, he was probably right."

The Mole fell silent as he remembered that bitter moment, for to him the venture had become rather more than the "jaunt" it seemed to be for the Rat.

"When are you off then, Mole?" the Otter had asked a day or two after this.

"Ah, we're not going after all, Otter. Ratty – I – we decided that perhaps this is not the best time."

How disappointed the Otter seemed, and how uncomfortable the poor Mole felt as a result, instantly regretting that he had so readily acquiesced to the Rat's wishes.

It was then that the Mole had begun to slip into that state of despondency none had been able to understand. What had begun as an impulse towards adventure had turned into a cause and purpose too deep and mysterious for him to share with another, yet too impelling to give up. A cause that he felt increasingly was for the good of the River Bank, though he did not fully understand why.

The one friend who might have helped him realize his ambition had declined to do so. Toad could not be expected to understand, and the Otter would not have been quite the same companion as the Rat would have been, sterling fellow though he was. Nor did he feel he could turn to the Badger, for he felt he would disapprove, and he felt so ill at ease with the secrecy that he and the Rat had maintained that he was unable to call and seek the counsel of his wise friend.

Such were the events that had led him to take his nocturnal walk, and deep was his silence, and that of the Badger, when he had finished relating them. Indeed, the Badger went so far as to open up his front door upon the night and take a stroll in the Wild Wood, that he might think a little.

When he returned he seemed to have come to some decision and said jovially, "I think that a glass of that vintage mayweed and elderflower wine you gave me on my birthday some years ago might be a good idea." He rose and took down a bottle of that famous brew of which the Mole was the greatest creator. "You remember the occasion?"

Indeed the Mole did, for he had declared, rather tipsily as he recalled, that "this is the finest I have ever made, and it should be allowed to mature for a few years till there is an occasion of sufficient importance that its quality and maturity will justify the opening of it!"

This splendid speech had been witnessed by Rat and Toad, Otter and his son Portly, as well – it was in the days before Nephew was on the scene – and the Mole had felt much embarrassed to have been so carried away by the occasion, and the drink, that he had dared say so much, and so portentously.

"I fear I was a little the worse for wear on that occasion," confessed the Mole, watching as the Badger prepared to open the bottle; "but if you please –"

"Yes, Mole, what is it?"

"Well, I am — I am not quite sure but —"

"Why, Mole, you look most strange."

"I feel strange, Badger, most strange. But if you please, do not open that *particular* bottle quite yet, for you see I — I do not think the time is yet right."

Mole slumped back in the chair as the Badger put the hallowed bottle back in its place, unopened. Mole looked more startled at himself than anything else, while the Badger seemed not at all displeased.

"I hope that great day may soon come, my good friend," said the Badger, pouring them out instead a glass of that good old standby, Mole's mischievous sloe and blackberry drink.

"And when it does," continued the Mole, "and it will, I feel strangely sure it will, then I pray that our friends Ratty and Toad will be here to share it, and Otter and Portly too!"

"*And* your fine Nephew!" concluded the Badger, raising his glass and turning their future wish into the present toast.

"Now then, Mole, I believe that we have some important things to talk over and we must not put them off a moment longer. You spoke a little earlier of the vision you had had of what we choose to call Beyond."

"Yes, yes I did," said the Mole, putting down his glass and leaning forward.

The two animals talked then for a long time, right on to the coming of dawn. Of much more than the Mole's vision they spoke, though of nothing that did not in some sense bear upon it, and return to it. Of the long history of the River Bank they spoke, of Toad's father; of the coming of the Rat, and the Mole's own quiet emergence from his own small territory into the wider world of the Willows and the River Bank; and finally, when the Mole thought all was said that could be said, the Badger began to talk of certain people, certain incidents and certain places beyond the River Bank – upstream of the River Bank indeed, which intimately concerned his own history – and explained a good deal concerning those old worn childhood books in the spare bedroom, and the small clothes, and the calendar with its fateful words "*The Final Date*".

The Mole now understood that the date concerned was the last on which the Badger had been able to hold any hope that he who had once worn those clothes, and he who had once enjoyed the books, would ever return to the River Bank from that place to which he had set off so foolishly, as it had then seemed: which was, which must surely be Beyond.

"One thing's certain, Mole," said the Badger, when they were finally sated with talk; "your voyage with Ratty will have to be revived. Your instincts in this matter must be trusted and acted upon!"

"But he is quite adamant," said the Mole dubiously, "and I could not possibly try to dissuade him from a course he wants to take and I have agreed to."

"Nor should you try! No, this is something that needs careful handling. Leave it to me and I dare say that Rat will change his mind!"

"Mole! Mole!"

It was the Rat's voice, and the Rat's knock, some days later at Mole End.

"Come in, Ratty, come in!" cried the Mole, opening the door, now back home and fully recovered. "You are most welcome."

"Now listen, Mole old chap, for I've something to say and there's no time to make a thing of it."

"Won't you even sit down?"

"No time for that," cried the Rat, going instead to the Mole's kitchen and poking about in his larder, his gaze not quite meeting his friend's.

"I think perhaps," he said busily, "that I was a little

hasty in withdrawing from the expedition – that excellent expedition – that you proposed in Spring. And so, if you are still willing, if, that is, you are ready and prepared to have me along, and to provide the victuals that our trip will require, then I –"

"But, Ratty!" cried the Mole, overjoyed. "Of course I –"

" – then I shall be glad, honoured indeed, to see to all matters navigational and nautical."

"Of course I want to go," said the Mole. "But it is *our* expedition and I could not possibly accept the role of leader."

The Rat shook his head and said, "I will have it no other way!"

"O my!" said the Mole faintly. "When do you suggest we leave?"

"Three days from now? Is that enough time to prepare?"

"More than enough!" cried the Mole, his mind racing with the possibilities, and feeling quite overwhelmed that the Badger could so soon have persuaded the Rat to change his mind.

"It is agreed then," said the Rat, still a shade uncomfortable as he turned back and went outside once more, quite unwilling to stay a moment longer, so much had he to do.

"And Mole," he said, turning and looking the Mole in the eye at last.

"Yes?" said the Mole.

"Next time I – I do not quite understand something, or, well – put my selfish interests before your own wiser counsel, will you be so kind as to do something for me?"

"What's that?" said the Mole, not at all sure that he knew.

"Box my ears and tell me not to be a fool! That should do the trick!"

He grinned ruefully, his apology made in his own way, and his amends far outweighing in the Mole's eyes any disappointment that he had caused.

"Three days then," said the Mole. "All shall be ready in my department, but really I beg of you, do not call me the leader or others might hear of it and get a very false impression!"

"I suggest we have our first planning meeting tonight at six o'clock, if that is agreeable to you," said the Rat, ignoring the Mole's protestations. "Otter will be in attendance, and Nephew has already agreed to take the Minutes!"

"O my!" said the Mole as the Rat hurried off towards the River, "O *my!*"

A short while later, when some rabbits came respectfully by saying they had heard he was about to lead a great expedition and would he be needing their help with matters of catering and suchlike, the thoroughly flummoxed Mole could not contain his excitement, but cried "Yes! Yes!", and the startled rabbits stared in amazement as that famous expedition leader performed before their eyes a jig of joy and celebration.

·III·
A Last-Minute Delay

"I did *try* – I mean I did *explain* to him – but you all *know* how he –" faltered the Mole miserably, looking first at the Badger, then at the Otter, and finally at the Water Rat.

"But, Mole," cried the exasperated Water Rat, "you knew we were planning to leave today. You've known it for days past. Why, it was you yourself who persuaded Badger to support our scheme, you who waxed most enthusiastic about it, and you who –"

"I know, Ratty. O, I know," said the poor Mole,

raising a dejected paw to try to stem the flow of the Rat's ire; "but *you* know just as well as the rest of us how very persuasive, very convincing, Toad can sometimes be."

"Toad! Humph!" expostulated the Water Rat.

"Trust Toad to get in the way of things," groaned the Otter.

"So it *is* Toad who's behind this delay, is it? I might have guessed as much!" growled the Badger, though with a certain twinkle in his eye.

"Yes, but what exactly did he say?" interjected the Rat. "Are we really to be delayed for some paltry and selfish reason of Toad's? The wind is in the south today, which will considerably help our passage upstream, and the sooner we —"

"It didn't seem paltry when he explained it to me," said the Mole with a trace more vigour. "And it's certainly not a matter of Toad being entirely self-centred, because, you see, we are all to be part of it. We need only be delayed for an hour or two and —"

"My dear Mole, you are beginning to confuse me," said the Badger, sitting down and taking out his pipe. "Why don't we all make ourselves comfortable and hear what it is you've promised we will do?"

The day was bright and breezy, fresh but summery. They were all gathered on the bank by the Rat's cottage, and it was plain enough from the pile of gear they had begun to load into the two boats moored there, that the Mole's expedition was about to start at last, and it was not expected to be a short trip either. One of the craft was the Water Rat's familiar blue and white boat, the other a smaller snub-nosed dory of the kind that can be safely loaded with supplies and towed along behind.

In addition to several hampers of varying sizes stuffed full to overflowing with provisions of every description, the bulk of which was food and drink, there was a large-looking tent, neatly stowed in a brown canvas bag, complete with pegs and poles. There were, as well, two large valises, respectively labelled in the Mole's neat hand, *Clothes: Good Weather & Evening* and *Clothes: Bad Weather & Mud*.

The Water Rat, it seemed, travelled more frugally than the Mole, for his valise was a third of the size of one of the Mole's and was labelled thus: *Clothes, of no value: if found, return to the Water Rat, The Cottage, River Bank, and if Owner missing contact Mr Badger of the Wild Wood.*

It was plain that their preparations were complete, and given the fair wind and good weather the Rat's irritation at their delay was understandable. The more so, perhaps, because his beloved River, as if sensing that she had her part to play as well, flowed full and majestically, her wind-ruffled surface catching in turns the white of drifting cloud and the blue of the summer sky, while on the far side the willows hung heavy with leaf now, green and summer-beautiful, their fronds swaying lightly in the breeze, caught sometimes at their lowest extremities by the River's flow, to be pulled forward a little and then released, then pulled forward once more.

"So, Mole," said the Badger, tamping at his briar before lighting up and taking a few calming puffs while the others, much under his sway, finally settled down, "why don't you tell us exactly what it is that Toad has said to you?"

"Well," began the Mole with more composure, "I do

begin to see now that I may have been mistaken in allow-
ing Toad to persuade me to agree to something without
first consulting you, Badger, and you other fellows. Also
I should have talked to you all a good few weeks ago
when Toad's symptoms began to show, but as you all now
know I was too much pre-occupied with my own concerns at the time – but let me tell you about it just as it
happened, and you can judge for yourselves! But –"

A look of anxiety crossed his face.

"What is it now, Mole, for goodness' sake?" said the
Rat.

"Well you see – I had not thought – O dear! I begin to
see that the matter is more difficult, more urgent, than I
had thought. You see it is not only what Toad said to me,
but what I suggested to him, and I did not mean it other
than lightly. Dear me – I –"

"Mole, old fellow," said the Badger, taking another puff
at his pipe and putting his hand on the hapless animal's
shoulder, "whether it be urgent or otherwise we can do
nothing at all till you tell us what 'it' is. Therefore –"

"But we should get to Toad Hall right away, before
he –" said the Mole, now seriously alarmed.

"So we shall, I dare say," said the Badger. "But before
we move from where we are, *please* tell us what happened
yesterday, and what concerns you so much now."

The Mole told them first of that afternoon in Toad's
garden and described how at the end of it a madness had
come to Toad's eyes and how, looking back from the
gate, he had observed Toad by the light of the setting sun
reaching for the skies even as he attempted to stand on
one leg.

They listened, and were naturally quite as baffled as the Mole had been, and certainly as concerned.

"You should have come to see me right away, Mole," scolded the Badger, not unkindly, "for we might have saved ourselves a good deal of worry and trouble both on your own account, and Toad's."

"I was overwrought with my own problems," said the Mole apologetically, "and in the days that followed I heard no ill news from Toad Hall, so really –"

"Be that as it may," said the Badger judiciously, "you had better tell us of this new development which is the cause of today's delay and your present concerns."

It seemed that the previous evening the Mole had been on his way to the Rat's to check a few last details concerning their expedition when – most unfortunately as he now realized – he met Toad.

Or rather, as he now reluctantly began to suspect, Toad had met *him*.

"Just the chap I was hoping to see!" Toad had boomed at him from the top of the Iron Bridge which the Mole had just crossed on the way to the Rat's house. Quite where Toad had appeared from he did not know, and it was only as he told the story to his friends that the thought occurred to him that Toad might have been lying in wait.

"I can't easily stop now. I am in rather a hurry," the Mole explained, trying to stride on. Talking to Toad could sometimes take a very long time, for Toad liked to talk, and he liked to know that others were listening.

"A hurry? On an afternoon like this? My dear fellow, whatever you are hurrying to do must be very important

indeed for you not to wish to pause for a moment or two and contemplate the joys of summer and of life just as I am doing. To think of past accomplishments and coming pleasures, to revel in the –"

"Well, I –" began the Mole, sensing that Toad was about to launch into some speech that might prove difficult to stop once it had started.

"But certainly," said Toad magnanimously, greeting the Mole's attempted interruption with a warm and disarming smile. "I would very much like to know what business could possibly be more important than enjoying a moment of peace and quiet before – well, shall we say, before an important personage arrives here tomorrow who might, had you not been hurrying off, have immortalized you, just as this personage will undoubtedly soon immortalize me."

"Immortalize?" said the Mole worriedly, for he instantly remembered that part of their encounter in May when Toad had mentioned immortality, and saw that the matter had not gone from his friend's mind as he had hoped.

Toad quite misunderstood the query in the Mole's voice, thinking that so great a word and so grand a concept as immortality was perhaps beyond his quiet friend's comprehension.

"Which is to say –" continued Toad, moving to the very highest point of the bridge, and puffing himself as if to embody the splendid concept he wished to explain. "By which I mean – made permanent; indestructible; known for all time; the object of respect and glory throughout the world from now till eternity. *That* is the meaning of 'immortalize', and that is what is going to happen to me tomorrow and the day after that if need be till the process is complete." Toad sighed deeply and added with seeming sadness, "And it might have happened to *you,* had you not been hurrying off on such an important errand!"

"It was not quite an errand," protested the Mole, beginning to fall into Toad's trap. "You see, Ratty and I have been discussing for some time now, with Mr Badger and Otter to advise, the mounting of an —"

"Aha! So the Water Rat is involved as well in this very important business of yours? And Mr Badger? And even Otter. While I, who thought he was a friend to you all, have not been included, nor even told."

"But, Toad, I certainly did not mean to imply —" began the poor Mole, feeling himself getting into water that was growing deeper and muddier by the moment.

"Well, well, let it be so, let it be so," cried the unstoppable Toad, with such a show of acceptance and resignation that an animal less kindly than the Mole would have seen at once that most of it was feigned. "Opportunities come to some, and opportunities pass others by. But certainly I rather think that if wise Mr Badger, whose views we all respect so much, had been aware that you so peremptorily cast to one side on his behalf and without discussion with him such an opportunity as I was about to offer, he might feel a little disappointed in you."

"But really, Toad, I —"

"Not to mention the Water Rat, who in such matters is always so decisive and practical."

"Toad, I —" essayed the poor Mole against the flood — no, the growing torrent — of Toad's determination.

"But no matter," declared Toad with every appearance of sincerity, and a rueful shrug of his shoulders. "I am sure you are a better judge of the strength of Badger's friendship and respect for you than I am. Let us therefore forget that I have said anything about this rare chance upon which you have chosen to turn your back, and talk a little about this business you are hurrying off to attend to."

"Well, it *is* quite important, you see," began the Mole, considerably discomforted by Toad's words, "and we have planned it over a long period, and after some ups and downs it is to commence tomorrow. But if you would just tell me what it is you feel I have turned my back on then perhaps we can —"

O, how slippery was that slope upon which Toad's "determination" had put the good Mole! How desperately the Mole felt himself struggling to keep a clear head and remember that the only thing that really mattered was escaping from Toad and getting to the Rat's house.

"O, this will take no time at all, Mole. Come and you will be persuaded. See and you will be conquered. Partake and you shall take that step towards immortality which, just now, I greatly feared you were rather hasty in rejecting!"

With that, and no more to be gainsaid or resisted, Toad gripped tighter still upon the Mole's shoulders as he guided him back over the bridge and thence through a small gate into his own grounds.

After a short distance much of the garden and the Hall itself could be seen, and the Mole was pleased to see that the grass that had been new-sown when he was last there had greened up a good deal since he had last seen it, and some of the plantings in the borders and the climbers about the pergola had begun to shoot and grow.

"You have certainly come a long way since that unfortunate fire two years ago," said the Mole politely.

"Unfortunate? Do we call Fate unfortunate? Some may, but Toad does not. Do we resist the tide of change? Most try, but Toad does not! Do we cling to the old? Everybody else may, but Toad does not. No, he grasps the new with both hands!"

The Mole felt Toad's grip upon his shoulder tighten, and was seriously beginning to wonder if Toad would get so carried away that either he would regard the Mole as part of the "old" and hurl him into the nearest ditch, or accept him as the "new" and cleave him to his bosom in even more unwelcome intimacy.

As he eagerly led the unwilling Mole back to the terrace where they had taken afternoon tea but weeks before the latter wondered with some foreboding how Toad might have resolved his dilemma of the empty plot, now that it was plain that he had not rid himself of his interest in immortality. The two were evidently connected.

"Sit!" commanded Toad, in some state of excitement.

The Mole obediently sat, looking up at Toad expectantly.

"Sit and survey!" cried Toad, standing to one side so that the Mole had a full view of the garden yet-to-grow. The Mole surveyed it for some time before saying (and never having been one to tell untruths or dissemble): "I can see very little; in fact I can see nothing at all."

"Exactly!" cried Toad ecstatically. "You see nothing because there *is* nothing. That's the point, the whole point, about the landscape architect's most excellent directive '*Client to decide*'."

"Ah," said the Mole.

"Nothing *yet!*" said Toad.

"Well, I really must be going," said the Mole quickly, struggling to rise from the chair into which Toad had put him, and hoping to make good his escape before the floodgates opened upon Toad's newest scheme. As the Rat was inclined to say, "The thing to do, Mole, if Toad is afflicted with one of his Ideas, is to get clear of him before the storm breaks, and let him huff and puff and dash around by himself till it wears itself out – or him out. Do not get involved if you can at all avoid it."

But on this occasion it was too late. Toad put a firm hand on the Mole's shoulder and held him where he was as he pointed to that troublesome vacant plot.

"The client has decided," he said confidentially, "to put *himself* there forever."

The Mole gazed at the place in question, and at Toad, and he pictured again Toad standing on one leg in the setting sun, and a doubt occurred to him.

"You could not very well stand there forever without getting stiff and hungry, and very cold in winter," he observed.

"Not *me*," said Toad triumphantly, "at least, not the mortal me. Mortals are mere flesh and bone and when we die we are gone."

Light was beginning to dawn in the Mole's mind, and with it came a sense of release. If this was to be the nature of Toad's immortality then the River Bank was safe enough.

"You mean – ?" began the Mole, beginning to describe with his hands a general form and shape that he imagined might resemble Toad himself.

"Yes, Mole, I do!" mistaking the Mole's dawning comprehension for a shared excitement for his scheme. "I mean to erect here the sculpted form of myself, which shall be cast in bronze and will last for many hundreds of years. That same statue, historic and memorable, whose title shall be Mr Toad of Toad Hall, shall be replicated throughout the world in miniature copies that others, unable to see the real thing, may have their spirits uplifted and their hearts warmed. Like –"

"Like busts of Beethoven, perhaps, which some keep upon their pianoforte?" offered the Mole.

"I shall be very like Beethoven, yes," agreed Toad.

"Or like those of Garibaldi," the Mole added with some fervour, for he himself had such a bust and it certainly uplifted his spirits to look at it. The Italian revolutionary had been the Mole's hero in his youth.

"Him, too, if you must," conceded Toad, who knew nothing of Garibaldi.

He pointed to the surviving pedestal upon the terrace of an old statue long since relegated to the scrap heap.

"Used to be four of 'em," said Toad indifferently, "but they fell into disrepair and that solitary pedestal is all that remains. They represented the four Virtues."

"I thought there were *three* Virtues," said the Mole, "Faith, Hope and Charity."

"My father created a fourth for my benefit," said Toad in a bored voice, "when I was born."

The Mole noticed upon the pedestal an inscription in Latin which read, "HUMILITAS SUPER OMNIA".

"What does it mean?" he asked.

"Nothing very much, I shouldn't wonder," said Toad. "I was never much of a scholar."

"You say that this work commences tomorrow afternoon?" said the Mole, returning to the plans for the garden, now very much easier in his mind than he had been before. If there were nothing more to Toad's scheme concerning immortality than spending some of his money in a vain and conceited effort to create a bust of himself, then he could see no great danger in it. Even Toad could not make such a harmless venture go awry, though he himself could not share Toad's belief that there would be a general demand for replicas of the original.

"This evening a continental artist of renown has agreed to come up to Toad Hall from the Town, and tomorrow that artist will conduct a preliminary sitting," announced Toad, pausing in such a way that the Mole knew he was expected to ask a further question.

Since he saw no danger for the River Bank in this new venture, wastrel and foolish though it undoubtedly was, the Mole was only too happy to oblige his friend.

"You suggested earlier that we – that is Badger, Rat and myself – might help in some way? That we might be a part of this – ah – immortality."

"You might, so you might," said Toad grandly, as if about to distribute largesse to workers on his estate. "I think it will be a good idea, and a gesture on my part in acknowledgement of acts of friendship in the past, if you and the others were to appear in some way in this work of art that I have commissioned."

"Appear?" wondered the Mole.

"In a supportive way," said Toad hastily. "Like those actors in a classic drama who come on and speak a word or two, or perhaps no words at all, but by their very presence help add to the audience's esteem of he who plays the hero's part."

"I am sure we would find no objection to that," said the kindly Mole, who saw right through Toad's pomposity (though the Rat would certainly grumble a little about it) but felt certain that the others would be willing to play their part in the harmless charade.

"It is agreed then," said Toad promptly. "Report for duty tomorrow afternoon."

"But Toad –" said the Mole, realizing too late his folly in agreeing to something that would interfere with the start of their expedition.

"You cannot, you must not let me down!" cried Toad immediately.

"Will it take long?"

"Minutes I should say," said Toad, who knew nothing of art and its making. "I have mentioned my idea to the personage who is coming and I have been told that in expert hands such a matter requires merely a few sketches. I, naturally, will be needed for rather longer but with you and the others it is merely a matter of seeing you and — and so forth."

"Well —" said the Mole feebly, now seeing no way out of the dilemma his own weakness and good nature had led him into, but feeling sure he could find some way of persuading the others to humour Toad, "if it will only take a short while —"

There were a number of other questions the Mole felt he ought to ask, such as who this "personage" was, at the mention of whom Toad's voice took on a strange tone of mischievous excitement which did not augur well. But the Mole desisted from further questions since Toad would take so long answering them that he would never get away —

"That's all, is it?" said the Rat irritably, now that the Mole's tale seemed to be finished. "We're to be delayed to satisfy this latest whim of Toad's?" He rose up and began to stow away the last few items for the expedition in the boats.

"I really do not think it too serious a matter," said the Badger diplomatically, "and as Mole has said, matters could have been much worse —"

"But that's just it," interrupted the Mole, "they *might* very well be worse! You see —"

"There's more?" said the Rat very seriously, turning from his task. "You have not told us all?"

"Well," said the Mole very quietly, lowering his gaze,

"there is something else. You see I felt so relieved that matters had turned out as they had, so pleased, that I made a most foolish remark. A remark that suggested something to Toad that he had not thought of before."

"You mean," said the Badger, putting down his pipe and rising up with a look upon his face quite as serious as that already on the Rat's, "you put a new idea in Toad's silly head?"

"Yes," said the Mole, very quietly indeed.

"What idea?" said the Rat with terrible calm.

"I do not know what came over me, but he pressed a glass or two upon me, as is his custom, and it must have gone to my head and before I left I found myself daring to suggest that – that –"

The Mole looked despairingly at the River and seemed to see in its great and sonorous flow not only the glorious eternities of life, but some of its unpleasantness and difficulty as well.

The others waited in terrible silence for him to finish.

" – that there are other, *better*, kinds of immortality than mere busts of bronze."

"Very unwise," said the Rat.

"What kinds of immortality?" asked the Badger in a very serious way.

The Mole hesitated.

"Well?" said the Rat accusingly.

"You must try to understand, I meant it for the best – on that previous occasion in his garden some weeks ago I had felt quite moved and wistful at the thought that future generations might see his new garden full grown. I felt it a pity that we along the River Bank, with the exception of Otter, have no direct kith and kin. I suggested – and, O dear, it was foolish of me, I knew it the moment I said it – I said that perhaps true immortality can only reside in the offspring we have, and therefore perhaps – O dear, I meant no harm –"

"Goodness me, Mole," said the normally cheerful Otter, voicing the worst fear that had arisen in the breast of each of them, "you were not so foolish, so *idiotic*, as to suggest to Toad that he should consider matrimony?"

There! The dread word was out and it rose and swelled and loomed above them like the darkest of storm clouds; and from the Mole's guilty suggestion it was plain that that was exactly the idea he had sown.

"I was speaking hypothetically," said the Mole defensively.

"But he took it literally?" said the Badger.

"He did," confessed the Mole finally. "He did, he did! O my!"

They stood in grim and gloomy silence before the Badger finally spoke:

"We must attend this artist's visit, and conspire to puff up as much as we can Toad's vanity and conceit in this sculptural enterprise. Perhaps the excitement of it all will distract Toad's mind sufficiently for this malignant seed Mole has most unfortunately sown in the over-fertile soil of Toad's mind to wither and die.

"But I think we may take some comfort from the fact that so far as I know there are no obvious suitors of Toad's hand in marriage hereabouts, and even if there were they would surely have the sense to refuse one of such profligate, self-centred, and unreliable character as he."

The Mole stared now at the Badger and then rose up to his full height and looked each of his friends boldly and courageously in the eye, like one who wishes to make a final confession before going to the gallows.

"There is still more?" said the Rat in a low and terrible voice.

"There is," said the Mole. "It is the nature of the artist whom Toad has commissioned to create the bust."

"Is he disreputable? Is he a marriage broker? That would certainly be bad," said the Badger.

"I understand not," said the Mole. "I understand the artist is of the female persuasion."

"Female!" said the Rat, aghast.

"And a female who has claimed some distant connection with Toad himself," said the Mole, making a clean breast of it, "if only at some very considerable remove."

"You mean this female artist is a distant cousin of Toad's, and herself a toad?" said the Badger gravely. "And it is upon the eve of the coming of this – this *Toadess* that you, Mole, of whom we might have expected something better, have put the idea of matrimony into Toad's head?"

The matter could not have been put more bluntly than that, nor the crisis more plainly stated.

The Mole bowed his head in shame. He had brought a grave crisis to the River Bank, albeit unwittingly, and the very expedition of which he had been so proud, so flattered, to have been leader, must now be threatened with postponement or even cancellation.

"May I ask," said the Badger in a voice made more dreadful by its measured calm, "what Toad's response was to this notion of yours?"

How slowly the River flowed by them then, how deep and dangerous its depths, how inevitable its coming, and its going.

"He thought," confessed the Mole finally, "that it was a very good idea indeed. In fact he —"

"Say no more, Mole," said the Badger, putting out his pipe at once, "for it seems you have already said too much. We must go to Toad Hall immediately."

"I shall go by boat, Badger, for to leave them here unattended with all our gear and provisions would be an open invitation to the weasels and stoats," said the Rat with a fierce glance at the Mole.

"I did not mean — I mean to say — I am sure that —" spluttered the downcast Mole helplessly.

"Enough of words," said the Badger, "reconnaissance of the situation and determined action to avert a disaster whose implications are quite unmentionable is what is needed, and needed immediately. Otter, you come with me."

With that, and without any further discourse, lest further delay bring the impending disaster all the nearer and more likely, the Badger and the Otter set off on foot, and the Rat got into his boat, leaving the disgraced Mole all alone and feeling as unhappy and as wretched as he had ever been.

"Shall I come with you, Ratty?" he said in a most pathetic voice.

"Humph!" said the Rat, grudgingly making room for him.

"O dear!" said the poor Mole to himself as he cast off the painter and the Rat began to row upstream on what the Mole still hoped might be the first leg of the expedition. It seemed a poor way to begin so noble an enterprise.

"Ratty – ?" he essayed a short while later.

"Better not say a word, old chap," said the Rat. "Best to stay silent for a while, for it distresses me to think of matrimony and Toad. Why, even the River seems nervous and fretful at the prospect. Best to stay silent till we see what damage has been done."

"Yes, Ratty," said the Mole in a very quiet voice, wishing they were already far, far away from the trouble and unpleasantness that he seemed to have created.

·IV·
The Madame

The exertion of sculling upstream, and the calming flow of the River all about them, soon put the Water Rat into better humour.

"We shall not let this matter delay our trip, Mole, old fellow, so please don't look so miserable, for it upsets me," said he, before adding a trifle grudgingly as he guided the boat to the landing-stage by Toad's boat-house, "I suppose any one of us *might* have made the same mistake."

The Mole accepted this olive branch gratefully and without further comment.

"I am not quite sure I understand why Badger is *so* upset," the Mole dared venture after due thought. "I mean to say, is matrimony really so terrible a thing? Might not Toad benefit from having to think of another, once in a while?"

"Now, Mole, be careful what you say," rejoined the Rat. "These are deep and difficult matters, about which neither of us knows nearly enough. You lightly mention, for example, 'having to think of another once in a while'. From the grim warnings I myself have received in the past I can assure you that matrimony involves thinking of another a good deal more than that, and the effort would certainly cause Toad trouble and stress and lead him to do something silly. We all know how much he dislikes gaol, do we not?"

"Yes, but surely —"

"Well, my dear chap, many have said that marriage is much like gaol, only worse, especially where a female is involved."

"I should think a female is generally involved if a fellow is to get married," said the Mole sensibly.

"Exactly my point," said the Rat as if to clinch the argument.

The boats rocked gently, and for a time neither ventured to get out, for the matter they were pondering troubled them and needed much thought.

"What we can safely say," said the Rat eventually, "is that the arrival of a female personage at Toad Hall brings matrimony nearer than if that person had stayed away. We can also be sure that Toad, who is weak and vain and capable of anything if he sees some advantage to himself, is likely to be vulnerable to the snares that someone of the female gender might set him."

"Are females *very* dangerous then?" the Mole asked nervously. The Rat climbed out onto the landing-stage and pondered the Mole's question as he tied up the boats.

"They are not dangerous in themselves," he said finally, "but I have heard it said that they have a capacity for causing trouble and dissension. I mean no disrespect to them in any way, of course."

"Of course not," said the Mole, adding ingenuously, "why, your own mother was a female, was she not?"

"I believe she was," conceded the Rat, a shade irritated to be reminded of the fact.

"Mine as well," said the Mole confidentially, glad to have discovered some non-contentious ground in territory that seemed so riddled with danger and difficulty.

"Perhaps it is enough to say that we along the River Bank have no need of females and have lived happily without them for a large number of years," said the Rat judiciously as he finally led the way into Toad's garden. "They are perfectly all right in their own place but perhaps they would feel uncomfortable here."

"I see," said the Mole, doing his very best to sound as if he did. For the Mole had fond memories of the female members of his family, and often, in his quiet and gentle way, regretted their passing. Life had brought him many blessings and many pleasures, but it was no good pretending that occasionally he did not remember his mother's touch with fondness, or that he did not feel wistful when he remembered the sound of his sisters' laughter in childhood days. Naturally, from the confidential conversation he had when he had been recuperating at the Badger's house, he had not forgotten that the Badger was not without a soft spot for a particular female he had known many years before and had never quite forgotten. So the Rat's seeming dismissal of all female virtues did not entirely convince him.

But perhaps the Rat recognized the fact and felt that some final statement was necessary to keep the Mole upon the narrow path, for as they approached the terrace steps up to the Hall, and heard the sound of their friends' voices, he stopped and put a hand upon the Mole's shoulder.

"Mole, old friend, you would be well advised to put out of your mind such dangerous thoughts as these, and desist from mentioning matrimony to those of your present friendship and acquaintance."

"Even my Nephew?" persisted the Mole.

He had some hope that one day Nephew would settle down and raise a family and that he, Mole, might have some little use and value still to a new generation. Not that he had ever said so bold a thing to anyone, least of all his Nephew, but it was no good pretending he did *not* have such simple, harmless dreams.

"*Especially* your Nephew, if you want him to remain happy and content," said the Rat firmly. "You must warn him against such impulses, Mole, should they ever present themselves. Keep him busy and occupied with things that matter, that's the best approach. Now, let us see how badly Toad is infected with this new idea."

The Mole judged it was best not to pursue his enquiries further, and they made their way up the steps, across the terrace, to join the others in Toad's conservatory.

From the warning glance that the Badger immediately gave them, and the air of weary good humour that came from the Otter, it seemed that they had arrived not a moment too soon. It was all too plain that Toad was in an advanced state of excited exhaustion and might not get through the hours ahead without yielding to a crisis of some kind.

He was propped up on cushions on a carved oak settee and constantly sighing and mopping his brow, which was scarcely surprising since the conservatory was very warm indeed.

"Pray close the door, Ratty, there's a good fellow, for the draught may give me a fever."

"I should say the temperature in here will give you that," said the Rat shortly, "if it has not done so already."

"Please don't vex me," rejoined Toad, sitting up a little, "for I have a very great deal on my mind and need a period of calm so that I may prepare myself for the ordeal ahead."

"Ordeal?" said the Water Rat. "I thought we had come for a preliminary sitting before an artist of some kind –"

A look of exasperation crossed Toad's face, and resignation as well, such as passes across the face of a parent who must explain something to a child who seems likely to have difficulty understanding it.

"This afternoon an artist, a world-famous sculptress no less, will commence an important undertaking in this very room, or possibly on the terrace outside. I cannot say. We do not put fetters upon such people."

"Certainly not," said the Otter heartily, winking at the Rat.

Toad thought he was sincere and declared, "You are a good fellow, Otter, and I will put a good word in for you so that you too might find some role, albeit a small and inconsequential one, in the great enterprise which is shortly to begin."

"That's very decent of you, Toad," said the Otter with a broad smile.

"Humph!" said the Badger and the Rat almost together, for both felt that Toad was making a great deal of fuss about nothing. Both regretted that they could not be more blunt on the point, but with Toad there was

always the very real risk of provoking precisely the opposite reaction to that intended. Who could be sure that the
wrong word said now, or too harsh a handling of their
errant friend, might not provoke so volatile a seed as the
idea of matrimony, which the Mole had so unfortunately
sown here at Toad Hall, into escalating and unstoppable
growth?

The Badger and the Rat were hardened campaigners
where Toad was concerned, and instinctively sensed that
to cast doubt upon the artistic enterprise Toad seemed
determined to engage in, or to belittle it in any way,
might very easily have the dire effect of thrusting the
"world-famous sculptress" he had commissioned into his
hapless arms. Nothing turns a fellow into the role of pro-
tector, not to say lover, more speedily than to suggest that
the lady may be less than she seems, and that his rising
affections might be misplaced.

Such a mistake can all too easily turn passing
acquaintance into undying love, and an unscrupulous
female can very rapidly turn a mere *declaration* of undying
love into a *bond* both spiritual and secular that only
death can put asunder. Though they had not talked about
it in so many words, both the Badger and the Rat
understood that this was the main thrust and danger of
the situation, and they knew that defusing it would need
some care.

The Otter was sitting comfortably nearby drinking
tea and examining with interest the pages of a periodical
placed prominently upon a low table. It was ominously
entitled *Ladies Home Journal* and its cover was so bold
in colour and design that anyone seeing it in a

bachelor's quarters might very well conclude that matters were critical indeed.

The forces of those of the female persuasion seemed already to have outflanked the Badger and his friends by placing such provocative literature under Toad's nose. For which reason, perhaps, the Badger was restless, and paced up and down by the huge panels of glass that looked out onto the newly completed terrace and the garden beyond, pulling out his pocket-watch at frequent intervals.

"Mole, my dear old friend, are you there?" whispered Toad feebly, affecting not to see him. "And you as well, Ratty? Come to me, for it is painful to open my eyes. Come nearer where I may more easily hear your familiar voices."

Toad was surrounded by potted plants of all shapes and sizes and he held a fan of Japanese decoration and design in one hand; with the other he clung on to the comfort of a spotted handkerchief perfumed with lemon balm, a resuscitative stimulant for invalids who have a social afternoon to survive.

They went to him together, the Rat showing signs of impatience, but the Mole with much concern, for their friend did after all seem ill indeed. Toad groaned a little as they pulled up chairs to sit by him, as if the noise of the chairs' legs scraping on the conservatory's tiled floor was almost too much to bear.

"O!" he sighed, and, "Aah!"

"But, Toad, you seemed in perfectly good health yesterday afternoon," said the Mole in alarm. "What has made you ill?"

"I am not ill, dear Mole. Rather, I am composing

myself and I beg you to do the same, for the Madame will commence the sitting very shortly. Pray tell me, Badger, what time is it?"

"Two minutes to three," answered the Badger indifferently, for something else had occurred to him: "You described your cousin as 'the Madame', Toad. You surely cannot mean − ?"

"Indeed I do," said Toad with great relish. "My family is cast far and wide in many climes and countries. My cousin, this famous artist, the *Madame*, is French."

It need hardly be said that this item of information, cast up so lightly by Toad, caused confusion and consternation all about. Dealing with an English female person was one thing, but a French female was something very different, and possibly far beyond their combined capabilities. Especially if she set her *chapeau* at Toad.

"When you say she is French," said the Badger very irritably, "you mean she is from France, and if she is an artist that means she is from Paris, perhaps, which the world knows is chock-a-block with artists and bohemians. It was not wise, Toad, or reasonable to invite a former enemy of this realm to −"

"O, you can be impatient with me, Badger, and you can scold me if you must, but before my cousin Madame d'Albert I beg you to be courteous and kind. She is a sculptress unlike others, who sees something where those who are her inferiors see nothing. Her gifts are legion, her talents formidable, and such works as she has so far deigned to give the world are −"

"Toad," said the Badger severely, "are you making this up?"

"I certainly am not. The Madame, suspecting there was a family connection between us, wrote to me and I wrote back, idly mentioning that I was thinking of commissioning a bust of myself. Great artist that she is, she responded immediately, saying that she wished to take up this challenge, and she has been kind enough to send me a copy of a magazine in which a great deal of space has been devoted to her art, and it is from that I quoted.

"Otter, pray pass the *Journal* to our doubting friend, or, if you will, read us a little from it to pass the time agreeably till she comes."

The Otter was only too glad to read aloud, though the Badger and the Rat would have preferred him not to, but having found the article in question, and that part of it Toad had just quoted, he proceeded thus:

> *Madame d'Albert, as she modestly prefers to be known, or Countess Florentine d'Albert-Chapelle, to use the title which her celebrated marriage into one of the most ancient aristocratic French families bestowed upon her, informs us that the Spirit of Art has long moved in her veins.*

It is easy to imagine the happiness with which the Badger and the others heard this welcome passage, for it seemed that she was already married, and unless the Countess wished to become a bigamist Toad was safe from her. They looked at each other with relief, and rubbed their hands with satisfaction. But no sooner were their hopes thus raised, than they were dashed back down to the ground by the passage that followed:

Following her late husband's demise, and discovering that all the family's fortunes had been lost in unfortunate speculations, the Countess decided to eschew her nobility and follow her Muse to study Art under the formidable direction of Monsieur Auguste Rodin, the Parisian sculptor.

Her remarkable "fall" from the fame and untold wealth of a French Countess into the role of an obscure étudiante d'art under a master whose harsh discipline is as notorious as his works are increasingly famous has only been matched since by her rise to an artistic notoriety that owes nothing to inherited wealth and social position.

Imbued with that selfless philosophy from the East of which Madame Blavatsky and her fellow Theosophists are the best-known proponents, which invites its followers to engage in charitable works and anonymity, Madame d'Albert is presently engaged on a world publicity tour. In the course of this she has become almost as famous as her mentor Rodin, all against her wishes, and wants nothing of the wealth, the acclaim, and admiring solicitation that her many male admirers wish to bestow on her.

"Simplicity of Art and a tranquil life are what I am — how do you say in your tongue so difficile — seeking for!" she says in English made charming and romantic by an accent that marks her out as coming from the country that has given the world haute couture, haute cuisine, and more recently the Eiffel Tower.

"Once I had all, but I had nothing," she says, "now I have nothing and I have all, so I am not sad for the old days when my late husband lived. No one can take the ache from out of my heart, so I am alone forever! Art alone is my love now; Art, he is my God; Art, he I most adore!"

"Is there much more of this?" asked the Badger who was stirred to an advanced state of agitation at these words, redolent of trouble and humbug as they were. "Not much," sang out the Otter cheerfully.

Madame d'Albert has spent the winter season in New York creating likenesses of those members of Society who have persuaded her of their sincerity in their affections towards High Art, and are willing to show their appreciation to her in a practical way. She never discusses the matter of fees, believing that to do so is to do a disservice to the Art she serves, but, as she has been quoted as saying, "to pay too little for that which is priceless is, as we say in my country, ignoble."

Now, New York's loss is London's gain, for Madame d'Albert intends to spend the Summer Season there, and sails imminently. Though we are informed that she has private business there, and intends to pursue delicate enquiries concerning relatives with whom her family tragically lost touch some years ago, we understand that genuine artistic commissions for execution during her stay will be considered, and applications should be made care of the Ritz Hotel, Piccadilly.

"And it is your intention to have this female lady staying here with you alone tonight?" demanded the Badger. He looked as dark and threatening as any had ever seen him. Only as he spoke did the Otter, who had read so lightly the passage that exercised the Badger so much, understand how grave the matter was. Never had anything so scandalous, so thoroughly dangerous, threatened the peace and tranquillity of the River Bank before.

"O, please, Badger, do not speak so loud or look so peeved," said Toad.

"Peeved!" thundered the furious Badger.

"My cousin Madame d'Albert has spent a night here with me before —"

A stunned silence met this astonishing statement for, if it were true, the situation was far worse than they had feared. The Badger and the others had been outflanked, outwitted and left very far behind by a loose French lady whom none of them had even met!

But the Badger was not one to let such reverses get him down. Where truth and honour were concerned his sword was mighty, and his determination formidable.

"You mean you have been conducting a dalliance at Toad Hall, and intend to continue it now under the guise of this 'sitting'," said he, advancing upon Toad. "And you expect us, your friends, who have done so much to help you in the past, to aid and abet this Madame, this Gallic strumpet, this —"

"I have indeed spent a night with the lady in question here in Toad Hall before now," he offered quite without apology, before adding with something of a mischievous glint in his eye and a shamelessness that infuriated the Badger still further, "but I cannot say that she made sufficient impression on me even to remember what she looks like. How should I remember so inconsequential a thing? And anyway, Badger, you really ought to know that —"

"Toad!" cried the appalled Badger. "You shamelessly tell us that a matter that has gone so far that it could scarcely go further, is merely 'inconsequential'!"

"But, Badger, how can I be expected to remember something that happened when I was so very young, and she was younger still? Indeed, by rights it is *you* who ought to remember it, for were you not a friend of my late father, and as a regular visitor to Toad Hall privy to much that occurred here in the years immediately before my birth? Might you remember better than I my half-uncle's last doomed visit here, when he came for a single night with my half-cousin Florentine, now Madame d'Albert, then but a few months old?"

Toad thoroughly enjoyed making this speech with its combination of revelation, injured pride and innocent childhood days, not to mention that it was all too plain that Toad had cleverly let the Badger dig the hole into which he had fallen. Indeed, the Badger was about to express his chagrin at Toad's shoddy deception, when he was interrupted by the timely arrival of Prendergast.

With a discreet "Ahem!" he appeared suddenly in the doorway that led into the conservatory from the main house, and waited for a moment before making his announcement. "The Countess Florentine d'Albert-Chapelle has sent her apologies, sir, that her toilette has taken longer than she expected and she wishes you to know that she will be a few minutes more."

"Aha!" cried Toad, leaping to his feet, the success of his argument with the Badger having served to effect a very rapid recovery of his health and spirits. "Tell her not to hurry on our account."

"I shall convey that message to her maid, sir," said the butler with all propriety.

"Quite so. When the lady honours us with her presence bring in some tea, will you?"

The Butler hesitated for a moment before saying, "I hope I have your approval, sir, but the Countess asked that tea should not be served till the sitting is completed."

Here the butler paused sufficiently to establish a note of disapproval. "She was quite insistent on the matter, sir."

"O, indeed," said Toad, somewhat deflated. He liked his tea, and knew that his friends did as well. "Well, I suppose —"

With that Prendergast slid discreetly away.

The Badger, hearing what had been said, felt a sudden surge of relief and hope. It was plain that the butler was not much taken with the Countess, and whilst the Badger had no wish at all to return to the days of wars against the French, he knew very well that in the normal circumstances of battle — those of Agincourt and Waterloo came immediately to mind — several battalions of French Countesses would be no match for a solitary platoon of well-trained English butlers, while in single combat there would be no contest at all. This, then, promised hope of a formidable ally in the battle to protect Toad from the French female.

"He seems a very sensible fellow, your new butler," said the Badger.

Toad beamed smugly and winked at the Mole. He proceeded to repeat the history of Prendergast's employment that he had already given in so much detail to the Mole some weeks before.

Toad's self-satisfied account of his employment of Prendergast — the others had been able to surmise rather more of the butler's reasons for taking the post than Toad himself had guessed — was interrupted by the chimes of a clock striking three, and the sound of the door into the conservatory opening once more.

"Gentlemen, the Countess —"

Prendergast's august and measured introduction was interrupted by its subject, who passed him by without a glance and began an extraordinary, and to the assembled males terrifying, advance upon them all.

She was undeniably an artist, for her dress was wild and strange, and in parts shockingly coloured, and so startling in its overall effect that it took some little while for an individual's eyes to pick out the details. To say that her basic garment was a utilitarian smock of the kind male sculptors habitually wear as they chip at stone or knead at clay is to do no different than elevating the cloth cap of the working classes to the shiny top hat of a prosperous industrialist.

The "smock" was made of the finest damask and very white indeed, and certainly not sullied by clay, or oil paints, turpentine or the dust and grime that comes with labouring over rock. Its brilliance was enhanced by the silken flowing drift of a white scarf so gossamer-light that it flowed out behind her like the fronds of an exotic weeping tree caught by a wild breeze. The rapid motion of her advance daringly revealed ankles clad in startling white stockings, while about her head was a scarlet turban of arabesque effect with silks and ribbons of many hues.

Her face seemed brightly lit, as if caught by rays of sun that shone through the panes of a gothic stained-glass window: blues and blacks about the eyes, rouges and reds about the cheeks and mouth, and the sparkle of rubied jewellery pendant from her ears.

Her bosom, which was of sufficient dimension that it was by some way the first part of her that advanced, remaining well ahead of her legs and arms throughout her entry, was covered with shining gold and pearls – a brooch, several necklaces.

"Toad, my love, my lost cousin!" she cried in a voice that was as loud as it was bold. "I am come back 'ere to you!"

Confronted by this startling and dazzling apparition, Toad did his best to stand his ground, till he finally weakened and sought to escape towards the Otter.

But it was too late. His cousin's reach was long, long indeed, and her grasp strong, her pull formidable. Toad found himself enveloped in one who was bigger than he in all directions, whose embrace was suffocating, whose cries of recognition and welcome were ecstatic, and whose perfume was dizzily overpowering.

"'Ow 'appy I am!" said she, retaining her grasp of the hapless Toad, and squeezing tighter still. "'Ow content! Already I adore you!"

"Countess – madame – cousin," gasped Toad, who felt himself beginning to faint in her arms, "I am – I am pleased – I feel – I – *help!*"

His half-cousin's continued embrace, no doubt normal enough among her artistic friends in Paris, was too much for Toad to sustain any longer. Feeling himself to be submerging in a sea of silk, face powder and perfume, and feeling it all to be so feminine, so unexpected, so delightful, and so plainly the harbinger of the matrimony the Mole had hinted he should pursue, he swooned quite away.

·V·

Summer Journey

The delay at the start of their expedition was not what the Rat and the Mole would have wished for, but once they had made their escape from Toad Hall and they had put Toad's troubles behind them, a sense of adventure and expectation soon came over them.

The afternoon was warm and sunny, and as the Rat settled down to some steady sculling, the Mole and he were able to talk, and to contemplate. At one time it had been thought that the Otter might have accompanied them on this first stage, and seen them set fair. But he felt keenly the parental ties that came with needing to watch over his son Portly, who, though older and more sensible than he once had been, still needed firm handling, and occasional direction.

Then, too, the Mole was unwilling to leave Nephew alone too long – the youngster who had come to stay with him some time before was certainly sensible enough, no doubting that, but he was very sociable and might miss his uncle's company, and so the Otter had offered to keep an eye on him.

But if the Otter's duties kept him at the River Bank, he still had an important part to play in the venture the two friends had undertaken. He and the Water Rat had long since fashioned their own special mode of signalling, which they used during periods of flooding and danger when all who lived in, on or near the River were on special alert. Their method was crude but effective – a twig of blackthorn floating downstream signalled coming danger, or beech to say that help was needed, and three sprigs of some common river plant such as water avens, or yellow flag, to indicate return.

In recent years the two had had little reason to use such devices. Life along the River Bank had been gentle and serene, and such crises as Toad created rarely involved the River. In consequence, the need for their signalling had reduced itself to the occasional cheerful warning from the Otter (up-river) to the Rat (down-river) that he intended to come down for tea or supper. Which gave time for the Rat to brew up before the Otter arrived; or if something more potent was needed then he had time to polish his pewter beer mugs and open up some fresh tobacco.

However, once the Mole had made his bold suggestion that they should fulfil their ambition and head upstream, the matter of signals and warnings had become a serious one. No one knew what lay in store, and though the Rat might have been happy to venture off alone upon the River, so conversant was he with its varied moods and sudden demands, the Mole was a different matter. He liked boats well enough, but had neither the skill nor the interest that the Rat displayed.

This being so, and the Badger being much exercised by the point, the Rat and the Otter had honed up their signalling, and the Otter had taken on the responsibility, with Portly to help, of watching the River for any signs that the Rat might send during their absence.

"I'm quite sure nothing will go wrong," said the Mole, rather alarmed by such precautions. "The worst I can think of is that the boat might capsize as it did once before, when I was learning how to scull, but I am a good bit more experienced in such matters now."

"That may very well be true," replied the Rat, "but we are venturing to unknown stretches of the River and it pays to be cautious. Otter knows as I do that the River is not always benign, she has her moods and fickle moments and must always be treated with respect – and then, again, we do not know what creatures live along the upper reaches."

"Much like us, I should imagine," said the Mole; "unless you think – ?"

He had sudden and unwelcome visions of creatures large, malevolent and strange, and began to wonder if the voyage was such a good idea after all.

"I do not mean to alarm you, old fellow, nor to suggest that there are monsters upstream awaiting us upon the banks, or underwater perhaps, that might cause us trouble," said the Rat. "Though I suppose all of us have heard the dread and ancient story of the Lathbury Pike —"

"Yes," agreed the Mole with a nervous nod. He had indeed heard that legend and did not like to be reminded of it. The pike that had the run of those treacherous and hopefully mythical waters was said to be malevolence itself. The Mole frowned, his doubts doubling.

"No," continued the Rat, quite unaware of how nervous this kind of talk made the Mole, "I am merely thinking that you should not presume that all animals live in such harmony as we enjoy down here along the River Bank. Elsewhere strangers are not always welcome."

"I shall certainly take my cudgel."

"And I the trusty cutlass that was employed with such devastating effect during our victorious struggle against the weasels and stoats to recover the old Hall for Toad," added the Rat approvingly. "We may not need them, but we shall feel better for having them nearby . . ."

. . . And there it now was, that weaponry, right there in the bows, just as they had planned it should be. They began to feel they were really on their way at last, and their talk was of the value of such precautions, and what clever animals they had been to think so carefully of all they would need.

"We need not go *too* far tonight," the Mole said; "just far enough to feel we are well on our way, and beyond the daily cares of the River Bank."

Such friends as they were had no need to debate such a point too long – when the right moment came they would set up camp for their first night.

Silence fell upon them, but for the plashing of the oars and the lap lap lap of water at the far bank's edge. The Mole could only rejoice that his longed-for plan was now finally underway, and recall how nearly it had come to grief, and why it seemed so important that it had not.

It was the compelling vision of Beyond that had summoned him, and of Beyond he thought now and all it might mean to them. Yet buried deeper still in the Mole's kind heart was the sense that he had done little with his quiet life and wanted, before he grew too old, to do "something" – to be remembered along the River Bank as having found vision and courage enough to journey forth at least once on an adventure which might prove an inspiration to others.

He himself was too modest, too unassuming an animal to think that he could ever reach Beyond itself, but perhaps if he got some way there he might in later years tell the story to his Nephew, and he – whom the Mole believed would one day be a much more able and adventurous spirit than himself – might find courage to go on further still.

"It is in the striving that we make progress, Mole, the striving –" the Badger had observed in the course of the nocturnal conversation that had meant so much to Mole, and had led to the resurrection of the expedition.

Such had been the source of the Mole's impulses and

dreams, and he had been much gratified that the Badger had not doubted him for one moment when he had said that he had an impulse that such a journey *must* be made. Times were changing, life does not stand still, and some future direction might be found in the course of their expedition. One or other of them must venture forth, the Mole had said, for if they did not –

"If we do not," the Mole had asked himself so many times since, "what then?"

He had found no answer then, nor did he now, as he sat so companionably with the Rat, as the gloaming began to settle in, and the boats creaked to the rhythm of the oars. The journey upstream had taken on a good deal more for the Mole than it yet had for his friend the Rat, more perhaps than the Mole himself knew or had been able to tell the Badger.

But here they now were – and if he had never quite told the Rat of all this in so many words, and how he believed that something beyond words might come from their adventure, it did not matter. Ratty was here *now*, not in some mystical and impractical future, and if there was one animal in all the world the Mole knew he could rely on in a fix, or when all others might have given up hope that they might come out of things alive, it was his friend the Rat.

Short-tempered he might be, irascible often, inclined to order a fellow about when he was tired but – well, there was none so dependable as he.

"What do you say that we stop somewhere about here, Mole?" said the Rat suddenly, interrupting the Mole's thoughts.

"Why of course, Ratty; whatever you say," said the Mole compliantly.

"No, Mole, whatever *you* say, for you are the leader of this expedition and *you* must decide!"

"Ah, well!" said the Mole, sitting up a little straighter and looking busily along the bank ahead, for a site for the first encampment.

"It will take us a little time to get our gear out and our tent rigged up," said the Rat.

"Well then, we shouldn't delay too long before we stop," declared the Mole. "So perhaps here would do!"

"A capital decision, Mole, if I may say so! Now ready yourself to leap ashore and hold us fast while I position the boats along the bank. I'll get the tent sorted out if you'll prepare some food."

And so it was the two friends began their adventure – with boats well stocked and well secured, their tasks agreed, their bedding all ready and comfortable, and, finally, good food in their bellies, and the stars to watch them as they let their fire burn low.

"Dear me!" yawned the Mole. "I *am* sleepy."

"Me too," said the Rat. "Time to turn in, old fellow."

"It is," said the Mole, not moving. "It is really happening, this expedition of ours, isn't it, Ratty!"

Above them the stars winked and shone, and somewhere upstream an owl called after its young, and downstream a family of voles escaped the surface to the safety of their nest.

"It certainly is happening, and it was your inspiration that made it so – yours alone. There's some who talk and some who do: you're a doer, Mole, you really are."

"Am I?" said the Mole, more sleepy still. "I certainly *hope* I am, and that I always will be."

In those first days of their journey the Mole and the Rat kept up a gentle pace, and used the time to settle down to the routines of travel, of when to move and when to stop; and, in the Mole's case, to harden his hands and arms to the exercise of sculling, for the Rat could not be expected to do it all the time.

That first night was the latest they went to sleep. Soon the rhythms of nature overtook them, and they rose with the dawn and bedded down with the dusk – whilst always making sure that when the sun was warm and their luncheon was over, they had a nap in the afternoon as well.

They talked and laughed as they went, and fell silent and moody if they felt so inclined, each respecting the other's needs, always putting their friendship and mutual respect before those minor irritations that any journey and close proximity brings forth.

True, the Rat was morose for half a day and sharp for the rest of it following not one but two near-capsizes caused by the Mole's poor steering. While the Mole, so rarely irritable, allowed himself to suggest that the Rat must be ... *idiotic* if he could not watch over the morning porridge for two minutes without letting it burn!

But such arguments and moods as these incidents provoked were as nothing against the many pleasures and discoveries along the way. Of these the greatest was that of the Mole's country cuisine – his stickleback fish pie was judged superlative by the Rat, and his water-cress soup garnished with butter flavoured with the roots of ramson simply *unsurpassed* – "and unsurpassable in my humble view!" the Rat declared.

There was a different excitement when they approached the Town and their route took them past His Lordship's House – that same great place upon whose hothouse Toad had tumbled from the sky, and within whose *best* guest bedroom he had successfully malingered in the lap of luxury for several days.

In view of the sorry memory Toad must have left behind him, they did not quite have the courage to go up His Lordship's drive and introduce themselves, tempting though it somehow seemed; but in any case, the baying of His Lordship's hounds was quite sufficient to deter them from venturing too far from their boats.

They did not voyage much further up the mainstream of the River after this. For one thing the banks ahead became built up with jetties and factories which gave off unpleasant fumes, and bridges over which noisy traffic passed. For another, the Rat's information was that the best route onward was not via the Town. The River on the other side of the Town, so it was said, was not really the *River* at all.

"It's easy to make the mistake of thinking that cannot be so," explained the Rat to the surprised Mole, "but you see in its upper reaches a river's true source is not easy to determine. Think what a headache the Egyptian Nile's source has presented to intrepid explorers. What seems a major tributary soon peters out, while that which looks at first no more than a stream, and may not even bear the River's name, may in fact become something vast and extensive indeed, and lead back to the source itself."

"I see," said the Mole uncertainly.

"I did not mention it at the time, for I was not certain till now that it was likely to be so, but I have good reason to think that that 'tributary' blocked up with reeds and barbed wire which we passed just before His Lordship's House —"

The Mole furrowed his brow and tried to remember what the Rat described.

"Otter's information confirms this, and ancient maps that I have seen suggest that it is so. Therefore I think that tributary is the way we should go."

"But the River seems so big here," said the Mole, not entirely convinced by the Rat's reasoning.

"It may be that the reason the River looks larger and deeper here is because it has been changed and widened by the Townsfolk, and made more useful to them. But after the Town it doesn't amount to much at all."

"I certainly do not want to journey on among these buildings," said the Mole, "or beneath bridges that make me feel uneasy, and if that other way will keep us in the countryside, among the sights and sounds we know best, then I shall be happier."

"I cannot say for certain, for no animal I know has ever ventured anywhere else but towards the Town just as we have done, but I rather think we should turn back and try our luck the other way."

With the current behind them, it was not long before they found themselves back at the mouth of the tributary. Seeing it again, the Mole was not surprised he had passed it by with barely a glance the first time, for its entrance was blocked by a tangle of old weeds and broken sedge

and rushes. Rusty barbed wire was stretched across from
bank to bank, overgrown with vegetation, except in the
centre of the stream, where the detritus of winter floods
– old branches and twigs, old paper and pieces of cloth
and a great deal more – had collected.

As they approached this obstruction they saw a painted
notice, now nearly illegible, which was strung up on the
wire and read: DANGER: KEEP OUT. *By order of the High
Judge.*

"It is a shame, Ratty," declared the Mole, not entirely unhappily, for the way beyond the wire looked dark and dangerous, "but plainly we can go no further. To do so would be against the law!"

But the Rat was not listening. He was using a paddle to steer and hold the boats against the heavy, silent flow of water that issued forth from the tributary they had found.

"Hold tight to the wire, Mole," he sang out, "for I want to take a closer look!"

He did so, first by peering down into the dark deep waters, and then, before the Mole realized what he was about, by stripping down preparatory to diving in.

"Ratty, I really wouldn't do that if I were you!" cried the Mole a little desperately, for if the Rat was not aboard he would be in sole charge of their vessels, and this was a responsibility he did not yet feel experienced enough to undertake.

But his appeal was all in vain, for the allure of the River and its watery currents was too much for the Rat to ignore: and anyway he was warm with sculling. With a cheery smile at the Mole he suddenly dived overboard, and quite disappeared from view, with only a stream of bubbles caught by the racing flow of the River to show he had been there at all.

"Ratty?" said the Mole somewhat desperately, for the flow beneath was strong, and seemed to be getting stronger, the boat rocking from side to side as he clung on to the wire.

The wire seemed to have a life of its own as well, for no sooner did the Mole put the full weight of his grip on it than it creaked and shifted, bent and gave, and the boat seemed to wish to slide away from under him. With a great effort, and using such power as his legs had – which did not seem much – he pulled the boat nearer and himself upright.

"Ratty! Come back!" he called.

No Ratty came.

Now the wire seemed to twist in his hands, and its barbs to seek out the vulnerable parts of his wrists and arms and prick at him, and stab as well.

"Ratty!" called the Mole again, now more desperate and more annoyed.

But still no Ratty came.

The boat, tugged this way and that by the second boat caught in the strong current, sought to shift from under the Mole again. Recognizing the danger and that his strength was failing, the Mole realized he must risk everything. He let go of the wire with one hand so that he could search for the painter which lay coiled up in the bows behind him and just out of reach, and clung on to the malevolent wire with the other.

"Ratty!" he found strength to cry out in the middle of this undertaking. "As your leader I order you to come back and resume your duties!"

The Mole at last found the painter and, leaving off the cashiering of the Rat till later so that he could attend to the immediate crisis, he struggled for some little while to ease the rocking, bucking boats nearer to the wire that he might pass the painter over and around it and secure it fast. He managed the passing over and around, but the securing proved beyond his competence, and the Mole had no choice but to cling on to the rope and sit as low in the bows as he could manage, his back to the clinker boards, and all of him aching and weakening more as the seconds went by.

"Ratty," he cried feebly from the nether regions of the boat, whose continued rocking and sideways slipping caused various packages and provisions to fall on top of him, "will you ever come back? I shall find it very hard to forgive you. *Ratty!*"

The Mole's desperation grew as beneath him, butting and scraping their teeth as they mouthed at the underside of the boat, less than an inch from where he lay, monsters of the deep began their dread work of sniffing him out, and demolishing the frail craft to get at him.

"Ratty!" wailed the Mole. "What shall I do?"

For as the monstrous sounds grew more ominous, and he seemed to hear the watery cracking and splintering of wood, it occurred to the Mole that it might be better if he released the painter and allowed the current to take the boats off down-river, safe from present dangers. On the other hand – and this was the Mole's dilemma – when the Rat reappeared, if he did (and here the Mole did not permit himself to dwell upon the possibility that the monsters had made a first course of his friend before making him the main meal), the Rat would not be pleased to discover his precious boats wrecked downstream and all their gear lost.

It was at such moments that the Mole rediscovered that courage and resource for which he was renowned along the River Bank. Quiet and unassuming the Mole might normally be, and very slow to ire, but only let the fates conspire to corner him, or to threaten one of his friends, and the Furies of his soul were unleashed.

"Ratty, my friend, if they have taken you I am too late. But if not there may yet be something I can do!"

With that the Mole heaved at the painter to pull the boats back up towards the wire and give himself more leg room, grasped the cutlass and stood up, as formidable and as ready for slaughter as any Viking who ever stood upon the prow of his ship as it drove hard onto an alien shore.

With his left hand gripping the painter and his other hand brandishing the weapon, ready to kill, he gazed into the depths below and saw the stirring, murky monster begin to rise.

"Avast there and may Thor be with me!" cried he, prior to bringing his sword down into the water below in the manner of a Nordic mariner fighting his final battle.

"No need to be too rough with it, Mole," a familiar voice cried out from behind him; "that old tree trunk will soon drift off now that I have freed it."

"Ratty," gasped the Mole, turning about and nearly tumbling in the water as he did so, "you are here, you are alive. *Where have you been?*"

Relief mixed with annoyance, embarrassment with fatigue, and the Mole could only collapse back into the bow and listen as the Rat took control of the boats and explained what he had discovered.

"The bottom of the tributary is as clean as a whistle, which means that the flow is good and there's better water upstream. I shifted that trunk out of our way and now we can just slide under the wire – how sensible and practical of you to slump down there in the bows, and to have shifted some of our gear and redistributed the boat's weight to ease my task."

"What about that notice?" said the Mole, falling back on the only protest he could make.

"O, that!" responded the Rat contemptuously. "Pshaw! No landowner has the right to obstruct lawful travellers upon the River, or curtail their freedom of passage. No Court of Law would sustain his case."

"Unless he was the presiding Judge," said the Mole, ever sensible.

"I would take the matter to the Lords of the Admiralty," said the Rat grandly.

"And the 'Danger' that was mentioned?" said the Mole, thinking perhaps of those monsters he had imagined were about to get him, and who might be lurking upstream still. The Lathbury Pike, for example.

"All stuff and nonsense," said the Rat, "and only intended to keep us from our lawful course, but effective only on the cowardly and feeble-minded, and not the likes of us."

"No?" said the Mole feebly, and feeling cowardly.

"Absolutely not," said the Rat. "Now keep your head down, for I'm going to punt us through with this oar."

The Mole saw the wire and its notice slide past above his head; he heard and felt the rasp of the dead stems of rushes across his shoulders, and he watched as the Rat nimbly negotiated these obstacles whilst still keeping both boats under control and guiding them forward.

"There," the Rat cried after a very few moments more of this, "you can sit up again now, Mole."

The Mole did so, and felt a surge of excitement. As the Rat punted on, the wire and its attendant obstructions soon receded behind them and were gone, and with them the River – the only waterway the Mole had ever known.

Now, ahead of them, hedged in on either side by impenetrable thickets and trees, was a different River, a deeper, faster-flowing one, whose ways ahead wound and twisted out of sight, and whose scents and colours were dark and more ancient than any he had ever known.

"O Ratty!" said the Mole with awe in his voice.

"Aye," said the Rat with new purpose, "now we must use all our skills and endeavours to survive, for this is new uncharted territory. Here we must be on our guard, and be ready for every eventuality."

"Hurrah!" cried the Mole, grasping the handle of his cutlass yet tighter and raising it in the air from sheer exuberance, for he felt now that the most exciting part of their expedition had begun.

·VI·
Cupid's Arrow

If Toad's sudden swoon into the arms of his friends was unexpected, it was no more so than the change that had overtaken him in those memorable moments when he had met his cousin, and she had met him.

Had his friends themselves been experienced in matters of romantic love and the speed, arbitrariness, and frequent unreasonableness of the attachments it creates they might have recognized the symptoms even as Toad cried out his cousin's name. For people not afflicted with the contagion of love do not cry out "Florentine!" with quite the passion, and the wild purpose Toad attached to it. Nor do they arise from their swoon, clutching their breast, and cry out, "Where is she? Carry me to her this instant for I am yet too weak to walk. Only the sight of her will restore my failing heart, and the strength to my legs."

And finally, for good measure, when his friends were beginning to suspect the worst but had not yet gathered their wits together to take decisive action, "Let me be; I shall seek her myself! Unhand me, you villains, that I may protect her from thee!"

Such, or something like it, were among the cries and pleas, the imprecations and threats, that the love-struck Toad uttered as he recovered from his swoon.

That he could not find Madame d'Albert was no great surprise, given his wild impatient state. She had felt that discretion and propriety indicated that his friends should tend to him rather than herself. She had no inkling then of what ailed him, and if she had done she would certainly have left Toad Hall and the River Bank, there and then.

Meanwhile, being the enthusiastic artist that she was, she took the opportunity of the extra time offered by his collapse to engage in a different project. She requested Prendergast to assume the posture of one pouring a cup of tea that she might sketch him and positioned him at the far end of the conservatory, where the light was better. But since that area was particularly thick with potted plants, it took the recovered Toad a good deal of hopping and skipping about, uttering his cries of love and hope, before he found the object of his desire.

She spoke first.

"So English, so *typique*, so 'ow you say, absolute in 'is formality! I like your butler very much!"

Toad eyed his man suspiciously and said, "Prendergast, have you a satisfactory explanation for watering the palms with tea?"

"Sir, I —"

"Then remove yourself," said Toad impatiently, "that I may talk to the Madame."

It was at this moment that the Badger caught up with Toad. That nightmare vision he had had when the Mole had first confessed the grave mistake he had made the day before had here and now, before his eyes, like a tropical storm coming from off the sea to devastate a peaceful land, become reality.

"Toad," growled the Badger in Toad's ear, "you are in danger of making a fool of yourself!"

"Love," cried Toad blissfully, turning from the Madame to his friend, yet still reaching a hand towards the one upon whom he had set his heart, "is a fool, a happy fool, and I —"

The Mole caught up with them and saw that the Badger was not quite handling Toad aright, and thought that he might try a different approach.

"Toad," he said, pleasantly but quite firmly, "I do not know what has come over you but you are in danger of compromising yourself —"

"I do not know, sweet Cousin," cried Toad, leaping up in the air and describing a brief pirouette with an energy that was gathering momentum by the second, "what has come over me, but I am in danger —"

The Water Rat now joined the *mêlée* and sought a better way of dealing with the bedazzled and besotted swain within their midst.

"Toad," he hissed, pulling him to one side, "if you don't come to your senses *at once* then we shall have to forcibly remove you to a place of safe-keeping till you have calmed down, and you will look very foolish in the eyes of your cousin. She will lose all respect for you and I dare say will cease the sitting forthwith, and her visit here, and what is more —"

"Ratty, old fellow, please don't grip my arm so tight, it hurts."

" — we will summon the police!"

"Not them!" cried Toad.

"And the Stipendiary Judge," added the Badger.

"No, not him!" whined Toad.

"And I should imagine that a bishop or two will be needed," added the Mole, following the Water Rat's approach.

"*Please*, not a member of the clergy," said Toad, now chastened, "for they talk so much and make my head feel tired."

It seemed that the resourceful Rat had indeed found a way to calm Toad. The combination of a great many more warning words like these, spoken in fierce *sotto voce*, and the continuance of that ruthless grip upon Toad's arm served to dampen Toad's ardour and finally to silence him.

It was in vain that the Mole and the Badger (while the Rat still held Toad to one side, and Prendergast was sent to fetch him a calming *tisane*) tried to explain to

110

Madame d'Albert the nature of her cousin's ailment; nor did their brief description of his chequered history, and his marked tendency to criminal behaviour, seem to make any impact on her.

"'E is *magnifique*, 'e is *formidable*, 'e is a toad *sauvage*," she exclaimed. "And now we must resume our sitting."

At least the interval of restraint seemed to have sobered Toad from the inebriating effects of that heady beverage of infatuation from which he seemed to have drunk so suddenly and so deep.

They thought it safe to allow him to speak again.

"Cousin," said he, "*sweet —*"

"Toad!" growled the Badger, seeing the danger signs once more.

"Cousin — madame," essayed Toad again, "I am better now. *I am in l—*"

"Be careful, old fellow," said the Mole in a calming way, fearing that another declaration of love was imminent. "When you speak to her, try to imagine she is a potted plant — that might help."

Toad stared at the Mole in astonishment, thinking that his words rather confirmed what he already thought: that the heat of the day and the airlessness of the conservatory was going to everybody's head. How else could one explain the fact that a sane fellow like the Mole could expect him to think of Florentine as a potted plant? What else but temporary madness could account for his butler affecting to water palms with tea that had long since dried up?

"I think, Cousin, that I am tired and need a moment's rest. Then, *my dear —*"

111

The Badger needed only to cast him a glance now to bring him back on course.

" – my dear Cousin, I trust you will discuss with me the pose you recommend for the statue you have agreed to make."

This was sanity returned, so much so that Toad drank the special tea that Prendergast brought, and out of courtesy had a peck of tapioca pudding. Finally he went out onto the terrace for the next part of the sitting.

The Rat and the Mole quietly took the opportunity to take leave of their host and return to their boats, with the Otter to help them on their way.

"Good luck, you fellows," said the Badger, lingering with the others for a moment; "I would come down to see you off, but one of us had better keep an eye on Toad."

On the terrace, Madame d'Albert was now able to turn her full attention on Toad. "Let me regard you, *mon cher*. Let me see you as you truly are."

Toad stood where he was, staring at her in some alarm.

"I do not quite know what you mean," he said.

"'E is so modest, monsieur, so like a bird that longs to fly but feels constrained from doing so," said she over her shoulder to the Badger, who by now had taken upon himself the role of chaperone and was rather wishing that the sculptress would be a little less flamboyant in her use of language, for it only encouraged Toad.

"Madame," hissed the Badger, "try to speak more simply, for Mr Toad does not quite understand your meaning. Regard him as being a little ill."

Then he sighed, for he saw that his intervention had done no good: the Madame had begun to flap her arms vigorously whilst running about the terrace, crying, "*Un oiseau!* A bird, a flying bird!"

How willingly and happily Toad followed suit. "A bird! That's what I am! That's what she means, Badger old chap! Isn't she delightful?"

The Badger frowned at this and let it pass. He was concerned by the reference to birds and flight, for he knew how Toad longed to do many things, flying among them, and how necessary it was for his own safety, and that of all along the River Bank, to restrain him. The constant constraints of his friends rather than self-restraint were what kept Toad from disaster – that the Badger knew.

Then Toad, exhausted, came to a heaving, puffing stop before the Madame, who had done likewise.

"Am I?" said Toad with hopeful obedience. "Am I like a bird?"

"A bold bird," said she, unknowingly feeding his vanity and love, even as he began to swell his chest and preen and parade before her like a peacock, "and a noble bird!"

"I *am*!" concurred Toad with sudden conviction.

"Is 'e not?" she cried, appealing to the Badger for confirmation.

"He can be," averred the Badger reluctantly, eyeing the strutting Toad with distaste, "I suppose."

He hoped that Toad might heed the warning note in his voice and calm down once more. He knew what little encouragement it needed for Toad to swell his chest, and how little more for him to strut about seeking to look as important as he felt. With the Madame encouraging him to think of himself as a bold bird, even a noble one, he had flown in a matter of moments from disappointment that his earlier declarations seemed to have gone unnoticed by her, to flights of fancy that gyred ever higher on the winds of her admiration.

"Where is my art to be erected?" she asked again.

"My sculpture? Me?"

"Yes," she breathed. "Show me, Cousin; show me *now*!"

With an extraordinary movement of arms and hands, much like a provincial actor making his first entrance on the stage in a part far beyond his range, experience and abilities, and driven by an impulse to wish to impress his audience, Toad strode across to the plinth upon which he so looked forward to seeing a sculpture of himself erected, double size.

"I shall be here eternally!" said he.

"O, Monsieur Toad, strike a pose!" she cried after him. "Be noble, be most bold! Inspire my Art with the immortality of your Spirit!"

Toad tried his best to do so, and after some experimentation – for despite considerable secret practice in previous days, he had not found it easy to strike a dramatic pose that did not very soon lead to fatigue and a loss of balance and dignity – he stood with his arms, hands and finally his fingers extended as nobly and as boldly as he could.

The Madame regarded him gravely for quite some time, and then came to a sudden and most startling conclusion.

"'E must be, 'e *is*, an Emperor," said Madame d'Albert with sudden decision. "That is what 'e conveys to me: nothing less than an Emperor."

"An Emperor," gasped Toad, feeling suddenly weak and faint, for it was physically taxing to be so bold and so noble of body for so long.

"And yet –" said Madame in a quiet and timorous way, as if some thought almost too awesome to contemplate had suddenly occurred to her, though the Badger suspected she had it all along, " – yet I wonder – Monsieur Badger," she said, grasping his arm and drawing him into the circle of decision, "'ave you never looked at your friend Monsieur Toad and seen 'im as 'e might truly be?"

"As he *is*, yes," said the Badger, finding that the resistance he was able offer through his greater height was less than the force she was able to apply as a result of her greater weight, so that he was drawn forward towards Toad and forced to look up at him, "as he *might be*, rarely."

"Then look now," she said with a grand gesture towards the perspiring Toad, who was now in desperate straits as he tried to retain his extraordinary pose and his dignity; "look, and what do you see?"

"I see –" The Badger was reluctant to continue, for he knew too well what he saw. He saw struggling pomp and blind vanity; he saw overweening pride and – and a Toad afflicted by passions he could not control.

"'E shall be *Imperial!*" cried the Madame ecstatically, plucking some laurel and handing it to Toad that he might hold it to his head like a wreath of victory.

"Imperial?" queried the Badger, peering up at Toad even as the sole leg that supported him gave up the unequal struggle and he began to collapse.

"Imperial Caesar, that is what Monsieur Toad shall be. And you, Badger, Rat and Mole, and Otter as well, you shall be legates, smaller than the Emperor, delivering scrolls announcing his victories! That is my conception. The sitting is over! Hail Imperial Caesar!"

This was clearly the conclusion of Madame's afternoon's work and it certainly satisfied Toad. He wobbled one last time and with a thump hit the ground, grasping her hand as he did so.

"Cousin," he cried, holding on tight and fatally deciding that her effusions were no more nor less than a declaration of love, "will you take the hand of Imperial Caesar in holy matrimony?"

The Badger stared in utter horror, but he need not have felt concern.

The Madame had had many proposals before this one, and though she had been slow to read the signals, now the truth of her client's desires was out in the open she knew exactly what to say and do.

"Cousin," said she calmly, "*mariage* is not possible for I love another."

"O misery!" said Toad.

"To 'im I am committed all my life."

"O despair!" wailed Toad.

"Also I 'ave other clients I must see *immédiatement.*"

"Which clients?" said Toad, still lying on the ground. He saw no good reason to get up.

The Madame pulled from her voluminous folds a list, and as she read it out the Badger could not but marvel at her skills and talents in the matter of love, and the subduing of a swain.

"My list 'as three names," she said, "but I shall sculpt them as one: the 'igh Judge, the Commissioner of Police, and the Senior Bishop."

"O horror!" cried Toad, miserably and in some trepidation, for he knew these gentlemen, and they were no friends of his.

"On my way back to Town I 'ave to visit the 'igh Judge at his big 'ouse and meet them all!" she continued ruthlessly. "Now I go," she declared, as sudden and wilful in her departure as she had been in her arrival.

"It is for the best, monsieur," she told the Badger just before a motor-car swept her away from Toad Hall's front door, "for I fear Mr Toad loves me a little, which is not good. So I do not stay."

The Badger felt a good deal warmer towards her than he could have imagined earlier that day.

As the Badger feared, however, Madame Florentine's sudden departure from Toad Hall caused her would-be lover a great deal of anguish and despair in the days and weeks ahead. Indeed, so copious were Toad's tears and lamentations, so loud his plaints concerning Fate, so dark and brooding his frequent silences, that the Badger felt it necessary to convene a meeting of those who had Toad's interests at heart, to discuss what they might do.

This committee meeting, which in the absence of the Rat and the Mole consisted of the Otter, Nephew and Prendergast, was held in the latter's downstairs parlour, for his master's demands were ever more frequent as his decline advanced, and he had to be ready to answer them. Prendergast himself was not quite as keen on this proceeding as the Badger would have wished, saying that his professional code demanded that he work only in his master's best interests.

"But you will help us help him?" suggested the Otter.

"I will certainly help my master, yes," said Prendergast with admirable ambiguity.

"Let us sum up the situation then," declared the Badger. "It is obvious that Toad's situation is parlous, and he is likely to become a danger to himself and others before long, if he is not already. I have little doubt that before very long, and despite the Madame's express wishes, plus the warnings we have frequently given, he will seek to escape the confines of his home to prostrate himself before his unwilling cousin.

"Failing which, I have the gravest fears that he is likely to be so overwrought, and his emotions so out of control, that he might well exercise that ultimate sanction upon himself from which there is no return.

"Or, else, and assuming that his natural cowardice and incompetence in such matters get the better of him, I hazard that once at liberty and continuing to be unrequited it is only a matter of time before he commits a serious offence, and is charged, tried and imprisoned for it —"

"Or worse," said the Otter, "since we all know that all

those other crimes of which he has already been found guilty will be resurrected by the Court."

"Therefore," continued the Badger, "I propose that –"

The Badger's proposal was interrupted by the loud ringing of one of the servants' bells. When they looked up at the indicator board on the wall above Prendergast's head they saw a flag showing Toad's desire to see his butler in the conservatory.

Prendergast set off at once, but had not been long gone when the other three heard further ringings, and saw other flags dropping down upon the indicator board, suggesting that Toad had set off about the Hall in a strange progress that revealed his wild and maddened state. He went successively from the conservatory into the drawing room (one ring) to the study (three rings) and thence into the hall (one ring either end) and then, most ominously, into the gun room (a small, feeble ring suggestive of final desperation).

"It is a cry for help!" cried the Badger. "But it is one Prendergast will be too late to see. We must go and save him from himself at once!"

Even as they set off there were more ringings.

"Wait," said the Otter; "he is on the move again!"

Then, most horribly, brought before their very eyes with the chilling remote swiftness of modern science, bell by bell, flagged room by room, they witnessed Toad's downhill slide towards madness and self-destruction.

"He's heading for the upper floors and thence no doubt out through the attics and onto the roof," said Nephew, and off they raced.

But in their absence, the bells continued their ringing

and revealed a different plot and twist from the penny-dreadful ending that his friends had foolishly imagined. For Toad turned back from the attics, descended via the back stairs, and, reaching the dining room, finally stopped and rang one final time.

It was there they found him, some coming from one direction, some from another, and the Otter climbing in through the half-open window (for he had thought that Toad might escape the house and make a dash for the River and there hurl himself in).

The master of the house was seated at the table, so far gone with despair and mental decline, it appeared, that he was unable to take off the covering from what seemed to them in their panic to be the gun with which he intended to end it all.

"Ah! Prendergast! At last!" he cried (madness in his eyes). "And Badger − (surprise) and you Nephew (puzzlement) and Otter, why you're climbing in through the window (mounting caution) in your eagerness to help me with −"

"Take it off him!" cried the Badger as he seized Toad's arms.

"But whatever −" spluttered the surprised Toad.

"I've got it!" shouted the Otter, hurling the dread object of destruction to the far side of the room.

"Really, I mean to say, old fellow," said Toad, attempting to rise.

"I'll hold him down," called out Nephew, setting to with a will.

"If this is a prank," cried Toad, struggling in vain against their collective might, "it has gone too far."

It was Prendergast who brought a measure of order andcommon sense to the situation. As Toad ceased to struggle and began to stare about rather desperately, Prendergast said in a measured way, "You called, sir?"

"I called for *you*, Prendergast, not for these interlopers, these unwelcome intruders, who —"

"Yes, sir?" said Prendergast very calmly and with a re-assuring smile, hoping thereby to calm Toad.

"I found my fishing rod in the gun room all right, Prendergast, but I cannot find the box of flies that go with it anywhere, nor even the reel, and —"

"You are going *fishing*?" asked the Badger suspiciously.

"I was hoping to till I was set upon so violently and you took my rod from my hand," said Toad in a hurt and injured way. "I thought it might help clear my head, don't you see?"

"Toad, I can't say that I ever remember you going fishing before," said the Otter, carrying the interrogation a little further; "why now?"

"I liked fishing when I was young," said Toad ruefully, "and I fancied I might like it again now I have found love. There by the calm flow of the River, to the mea-sured rhythm of the cast, I shall weave a poem about the lady who has left me —"

The animals exchanged serious and meaningful glances but let him continue.

"You see, Badger, she inspires in me moods and mem-ories long forgotten. No doubt you remember these lines of the hapless lover:

> *Distracted with Care,*
> *For Florentine the Fair;*

Since Nothing cou'd move her,
Poor Toady, her Lover,
Resolves in Despair
No longer to languish,
Nor bear so much Anguish;
But, mad with his Love,
To –"

Having already substituted Florentine for the original Phyllis, and himself for Damon, it had been Toad's intention to continue the poem with a few lines about fishing. Unfortunately, the Badger was rather losing patience and tried to interrupt him, but Toad, always relishing an audience, and always glad to shock others if he could, made the grave – the very grave – mistake of continuing the poem as originally written:

"But, mad with his Love,
To a Precipice goes!"

Here Toad raised his voice, and rolled his eyes in semblance of a madman before uttering the mordant final lines:

"Where a Leap from above
Wou'd soon finish his Woes!

"Of course," said Toad immediately, "I do not mean –"
"No, Nephew, do not release him quite yet," commanded the Badger very seriously, not seeing the joke at all. Though reassured somewhat by Toad's generally calm tone, he feared it might indicate that he had reached a benign phase of his ailment which might be of only short

duration before something more violent took him over once more. A theory surely amply confirmed by the last lines of the ditty Toad had spoken.

"We feel, Toad old chap," said the Badger, trying to sound at once pleasant but firm, "that for your own good it would be wise if you were confined —"

"For my own good!" cried Toad, enraged.

The Badger sighed, for it was plain that the benign phase was indeed to be but short-lived.

"Confined, yes; but you shall be granted all the comforts you need —"

"But I pay for them!" shouted Toad, struggling once more, and beginning to see the dangerous drift of the conversation. "They're mine!"

" — for so long as it may take for this — this aberration —"

"Of course love's an aberration, you dunderhead!" yelled Toad, suddenly laughing wildly. "It's wonderful, it's confusing, and it makes my head ache. Therefore a quiet spot of fishing and —"

" — this delusive impulse —"

Toad was suddenly still, seeing that struggling did not help and only exhausted him.

"So what shall you do to me?" said he, plaintive now.

The Badger saw that the cycle of madness was almost complete and that their charge was declining into depression and gloom once more.

"We shall confine you to your bedroom and fetch a doctor who shall prescribe a sedative till you are fully recovered."

"Please, Badger," cried Toad suddenly, hurling himself

from Nephew's grasp and falling to his knees, "do not do this to me. I cannot bear incarceration! I cannot stomach having my liberty taken away! Have mercy upon me!"

As he was pleading thus, the Badger came forward to him, much moved by his despair. No animal likes to imprison another, no friend to cramp another's freedom.

"Alas, Toad," said the Badger, "we are all friends here and can speak openly. We fear a return in you of that wildness and behaviour that landed you in such trouble and caused you so much misery in the past, and we are pledged to protect you from your own weaknesses. If Mole and Ratty were here they would say the same."

"O, I see that you are right!" said Toad pathetically. "But woe is me that I seem to have found happiness only to know despair!" He began weeping and sobbing even more than before as his friends sought to comfort him.

In the middle of this, and sobbing still, Toad managed to catch the eye of Prendergast who was standing a little aloof, and somewhat embarrassed; and catching his eye Toad winked, and then winked again.

"Dear Badger, and you, thoughtful Otter, O, and you too, Nephew, I am sorry I have caused you grief and misery. I have been mad with love and grief, it is true. No doubt I am my own worst enemy and ought to be confined as you suggest. I will willingly do as you say, but may I ask one small favour?"

With Toad so plainly contrite and more at peace with himself, and accepting the necessity of the course of action they suggested, they had released their hold of him a little. Sufficiently so for him to rise in their midst as he talked – though holding his head low and with his shoulders bowed – while he kept a quizzical eye upon Prendergast.

"Of course, old friend," said the Badger, "if there is a favour we can grant –"

"Prendergast, that item we put in storage when you first arrived?"

"Yes sir," said Prendergast coolly, understanding at once the nature of his master's request. O, how his spirit soared at all these goings-on! How much more exciting this was than His Lordship's House. True, down there in his par-

lour he had weakened for a time, and seemed to favour the enemies of his master. But now, seeing the glorious Mr Toad's courageous attempts to fend off his foes and ene- mies and make good his escape, how could he not aid and abet him?

"Is it ready for its first outing?" Toad asked.

Mr Toad was, of course, speaking of the powerful

motor-launch that had been secreted in the boat-house.

"Quite ready, sir."

"Is this something I can fetch for you, Toad?" asked the Otter all unsuspectingly.

"Dear fellow," said Toad faintly, "that will not be necessary. Prendergast here has reassured me on a small domestic matter and now I am ready —"

He righted himself at last, he looked them bravely in the eye, and suddenly he was no abject and sorry Toad, but a Toad Imperial, a Toad Immortal.

"Why, Toad, you look a good deal better now you have accepted the wisdom of our advice," said the Badger with satisfaction. "Now come along —"

"I've never been better!" cried Toad, pushing the Otter suddenly back a step or two and the Badger sideways before, stooping low to grab the fishing rod, he leapt towards the open window.

"Toad, you deceitful creature!"

"Ha!" cried Toad, warding them off with the rod. "Confine me again, would you? Imprison me? For my own good, eh? Prendergast, I order you to lock that door upon these villains while I —"

With a nimble leap Toad was up and out of the window and had slammed it shut and thrust a nearby rake against the window jamb to make it impossible to open from inside.

Then, as they shouted out their warnings and their rage, and sought in vain to open the window and the door that Prendergast had quickly locked, Toad scampered across the terrace and made towards the boat-house.

But not in so much haste or panic that he did not find time to pause at that spot where she he loved had elevated him to the status of Imperial Caesar, and there raise himself up in that imperious pose once more, while casting a backward glance of considerable satisfaction at the faces of his confined, imprisoned and incarcerated do-gooding friends.

"I am imperial indeed!"

"Sir!" called Prendergast from the terrace, where he had hurried to help his master. "I fear it will not be long before they make good their escape. You will find the rest of the fishing tackle you were seeking in the boat, along with a rod which I judged better for boat fishing."

"But aren't you coming with me, Prendergast? That's your job, isn't it? I order you to, now!"

"Ah, sir, would that I could, but it is against my professional code, I fear. Butlers may under the second part of the fourth Schedule of the Servants Act of 1899 aid their masters, but they may not abet. I have done the first, sir, to the best of my ability, but the second is beyond my conscience. I shall keep the house in good order against the day when you return home!

"I shall also prepare everything for that Grand Opening which I believe it is your intention to hold in early autumn."

"But, Prendergast – I do not know how to drive the boat!"

"It is a modern craft, sir. Simply crank the engine with

the implement all ready by the wheel, make sure you cast off the ropes, and turn sharp right, very sharp right, as you exit the boat-house. It is as easy, if I may make the analogy, as driving a motor-car or piloting a flying machine, at which I believe you have considerable experience. Now, sir, it sounds as if your guests have escaped –"

With these words of advice and farewell, Prendergast sent Toad on his way and watched with considerable pleasure as his master reached the boat-house. And even more pleasure when a short time later, with his pursuers already crossing the lawn and about to reach him, there was the roar of an engine, and his master's new launch shot out of the boat-house. It headed erratically towards the far bank of the River, before turning sharply right, then it was gone in a welter of smoke and spray, upstream towards His Lordship's House in pursuit of Madame d'Albert.

"May I wish you the very best of luck, sir," said the excellent Prendergast, adding, as much to himself as in any hope that Toad could possibly hear, "and if you need me I shall be here at the Hall ever at your service."

But it was Toad, far off now and unseen, who had the final word. Perhaps, after all, he heard Prendergast's kind words and wished to acknowledge them; or, possibly, he wished to remind his well-meaning but unwise friends that, while it was true that the course of true love never runs smooth, it is also generally agreed that love conquers all.

Therefore, beginning to gain confidence in the handling of his boat, and seeing a cord dangling down above the wheel, he tugged at it twice and was gratified to hear the sound it made: "Toot! Toot!"

"Ha ha!" cried Toad happily. "I *am* as clever as I look, and as brilliant as I seem! I am on my way at last to capture my love's heart and make her mine!"

Toot! Toot!

·VII·
At the Sign of the Hat and Boot

The weeks that followed the Rat and the Mole's decision to continue their journey by way of the tributary they had discovered, were among the most exciting and happiest the Mole could remember, amply fulfilling his early expectations of the expedition.

The Rat, being a practical animal little given to expressions of sentiment, was disinclined to speak in dramatic terms, preferring at the end of each day's doings to sum things up with brief phrases such as "that was a close

shave" and "not for the faint-hearted" or, as was sometimes the case, "a rum go".

As for happiness, he confined its expression to pleasur-
able sighs and agreeable silences, with, on a very few
occasions, the addition of some such sentiment as, "Well
Mole, old fellow, I think this is proving to be well worth-
while."

On rarer occasions still the Rat would forget himself
and make up a shanty-like song, just as he had in his
younger days when the Mole first knew him, and half
hum and half sing it, with words to match the mood and
moment.

The Mole had none of the Rat's reservations and, apart
from the "close shaves", he expressed his pleasure and joy
at the many things they saw and did, and chatted away
most contentedly when the day was done and they were
preparing their encampment for the night.

The country they passed through was hillier than they
were used to, and more given to undergrowth and heath,
and the River's flow was a little faster. Here and there
where its turns were sharp, deep pools had formed whose
cold and peaty depths yielded little to the sun, remaining
opaque and mysterious. In such places the air could be
chill and dank, and where the bank was tangled and overgrown there was a permanent impression of evening
coming, even on a sunny day.

"We've not yet gone as far as you might think, Mole.
That's because we can't see much beyond the banks, and
the River's route twists and turns a good deal here, giving
a false impression of distance travelled," he explained a
few days into this phase of the journey.

The Rat had to navigate with care, for such was the flow of the water, and the sudden turns in its course, that they could quite suddenly find themselves beset by gusting, fluky winds, on waters whose surface was rough and choppy, and whose currents had a will of their own. For this reason, and because in the Rat's view the River was beginning to have about it the smell of coming challenge and even danger, they proceeded slowly, and on some days chose to stay where they were.

Once they reached more open countryside they saw no purpose or pleasure in hurrying along and seeing nothing, especially as the weather had turned hot. The bank was hardening and drying as they went, and they took care to moor their craft out of the sunshine, lest their provisions suffer too much from the heat, their butter grow rancid, and the water they carried become too warm to be refreshing.

The Mole, the expedition's cellarman as well as victualler, adopted a variety of devices to keep things cool – his first duty on stopping being to lower certain of the provisions into the water, wrapped in waterproof paper where necessary, and attached by string for easy retrieval.

They also took care to set their camp in such a way that they could keep a good eye on all of it at all times. They had heard that the weasels and stoats they were likely to come across were even more rough and treacherous than those they knew from the Wild Wood.

"Be careful, Ratty," the Otter had warned, "my grandfather told me that many a traveller who voyaged as far as the upper reaches never came back to tell their tale –"

They had a goodly stock of dry goods and iron rations

set aside against emergencies, and when their initial supply of fresh produce ran out, they did their best to maintain a varied diet. It was the season of salads and fresh green growth, and the Mole could not pass a clump of mint or a raft of water-cress without pausing awhile to put some by to have with their meal later in the day.

Fresh dairy produce proved more difficult to find, and for a week or two they had none at all. But just when they were beginning to despair of ever tasting milk again, the River came to the end of its run through uninhabited heathland and brought them to a farm with a water-driven mill. Here they were made welcome and most comfortable for two nights in a barn, the farmer being away for a day or two on business, and his wife and daughter more than content to entertain the travellers.

They were amused to find that stories of the River Bank and its inhabitants were well known in those parts, and in particular of the "famous Mr Toad of Toad Hall".

"You mean the infamous and notorious Mr Toad, do you not?" said the Rat, thinking they had made some mistake.

"Indeed not, sir," responded the farmer's wife heartily, "and you must be thinking of a different gentleman to call him so. Why, Mr Toad single-handedly saved the Town from destruction with his courage and skill at the controls of the flying machine he bravely piloted –"

"I really must protest –" began the Rat before the Mole restrained him and let their hostess continue.

"Aye, you're right, sir," said she warmly; "I should have said *very* bravely, should I not?"

"Indeed," said the Mole, his restraining hand on the Rat's arm still firm.

"But then again," said her daughter, "the tale I like about that Mr Toad is how he lived for several months with the High Judge, not letting on who he was at all. All free and for nothing!"

"That was clever and cunning, that was, and whereas some might say it weren't right to do as he did, others would say that that High Judge – O, he's a terrible cold man, he is, and do stand so on his rights – had it coming to him. And so you say you know Mr Toad, and he might even recognize you if he passed you by in his motor-car?"

"He hasn't got a –"

"He certainly would," said the Mole before the Rat could spoil things, "though, of course, he's far too busy and important to have time to say hello to common folk like us!"

"Now that's a pity," rejoined the farmer's wife confidentially, "for I always say if folk can't find time to pass the time of day there's summat wrong with the way they're living. 'Course, in the old days we got a lot more boats and craft up this way but then they built that canal, and His High Judgeship blocked up the entrance to the River –"

"You do call this part the River then?" said the Rat, for the point had taxed them somewhat.

"Indeed we do. That shallow stagnant pond of a thing they call the River down Town way is nothing of the sort and never was. No, if it's the real River you're after, then you're on the right track here. Mind you –"

Her face darkened.

"Yes?" queried the Water Rat, always eager for information about the River and its ways.

"Well, I've no need to say it to a knowledgeable nautical gentleman like you, sir, but you'll not be taking the craft past the Hat and Boot Tavern up Lathbury way, will you?"

"And why not?" asked the Mole, who rather feared he already knew the answer.

"You mean you don't know?" she replied, taken aback.

"Why that *particular* tavern?" said the Rat.

"Well, they'm in a better position to answer that, sir, if they've a mind to talk about it –"

" – or talk at all," added her daughter with a meaningful look.

"You wouldn't mind telling us, would you?" said the Mole.

"It's not summat us around here talk a lot of – I only mentioned it 'cos I thought you knew already. You ask at the Hat and Boot, they'll –" She busied herself about the place, plainly unwilling to say more.

Recognizing that it was time to press on with their journey, the Rat and the Mole took their leave and, laden with fresh supplies, made their way back to their boats. But as they were casting off, the farmer's daughter came down to see them with some sandwiches she had made wrapped up in cloth tied with a ribbon.

"I'm sorry my Ma went quiet an' that but she comes from Lathbury way herself and don't talk of such things, like a lot of her generation."

"Is there really danger ahead?" asked the Rat. "Is that what she meant?"

"Not up as far as the Tavern there ain't," said she, "but I wouldn't venture further 'n that, not in so frail a craft as this, any road."

"No?" said the Rat. "We were thinking –"

A look of alarm came into the young girl's eyes.

"Don't think of goin' further, promise you won't, 'cos she'll have you for supper as quick as a flash."

"Who will?" said the Mole, very much fearing that he already knew.

"The Lathbury Pike, sir," said she in a very hushed and fearful voice. "She be active again."

As they thanked her for the sandwiches, and the advice, and set off up the River once again, they heard her final despairing call:

"Don't go up past the Tavern, sirs; I wish you'd promise you wouldn't!"

The Mole and the Rat waved, and called reassuringly back, but they made no promises, for if an expedition curtailed itself at mere speculation and rumour, or on the basis of local fears and superstitions, nowhere in the world that was backward and uncivilized would have ever been explored.

Their journey now took them past a series of deserted villages – some no more than raised terraces of grass across which sheep and cow now grazed, others more substantial affairs of broken homesteads and the ruins of ecclesiastical buildings and old factories of bygone times, with broken chimneys, boiler rooms, and rusting iron that lay where it had fallen or been piled decades before.

Then too there were ancient woods through which the water course wound its lonely way, whose decayed and once-pollarded trees and acres of uniform younger growth spoke of a time when the woodland crafts were practised more than they were now. Here charcoal burners had once worked in the summer months, and basket makers had cut the osiers and sedges and stacked them up to dry.

Old jetties, rotten now, were collapsing into the water, and here and there a thick-planked wooden barge was pulled up onto the bank, or lay half in the water and half out, far beyond the hope of salvage.

Yet never once did this ruin and decay seem gloomy or depressing to the two enterprising explorers. For nature was busily in the process of claiming back what had once been taken and then abandoned, and in the very decay and ruin of what they saw was new growth, the green

shoots of new life yet to come. As in an old barge they passed, its split and broken prow glorious with the shining yellow blooms of marsh marigold; and the bank of a deserted railway near which they made their camp for three whole days, which was home to bats and sand martins, which flew and squeaked and made merry by dusk and by dawn.

As for the once-worked woodlands that they found, the gaps where trees had been felled were filling up already, and the piles of wood spoil rotting back to earth.

"Look there!" cried the Mole with much delight, pointing again and again that the Rat might share his pleasure.

But it was not the broken bricks of some small mill he pointed at, but the honeysuckle that grew now in between, whose dew-dropped blooms caught the morning sun; not the old bridge that arced across their riverway that he meant the Rat to see, but the ragwort that clung now to the mortar of the bricks and competed with the bramble that was spreading all along; not even the rusting gate that blocked a forgotten bridle path through a forgotten field, but the blackbird that perched atop it, and the butterflies that tumbled in amongst the vivid purple blooms of the lilacs that already sought to push the gate aside forever.

These were halcyon days that the Mole never wanted to end. At a particularly peaceful and contented moment he finally told the Rat something of his memorable conversation with Badger when he was convalescing.

His friend said little, preferring to listen in silence as was his wont, staring into the shadows and at the setting sun, nodding his head and now and then filling his pipe once more. This was the Rat's way with such matters, and the Mole understood it well.

"Moly," said he at last, "you made mention of these items of clothing, a calendar and such like in Badger's spare room. What of them? What did they represent?"

Just like Ratty, thought the Mole to himself wryly, to say nothing for so long and then to go right to the heart of the matter.

"I confess," replied the Mole, "that I have often wondered whether I should speak of this, for there was a certain confidentiality about our talk, but – Badger said that I might do so when the time was right. I know not what lies ahead of us, Ratty, but as I have said from time to time, for me there has been about this expedition of ours a desire to get a little nearer to the mystery we have called Beyond.

"I know that in the past when we have ventured towards that mystery there has been a degree of risk and chance involved, and the sense of crossing over from one world to another – a journey from which, one day, we shall not return. You have said before tonight that you sensed a certain danger about this journey, and that we who make it, and our friends who helped us prepare for it and wished us well of our undertaking, must accept there might be risks involved.

"I will only say now that I sense that in the days immediately ahead those risks may be nearer –"

"I have had the same feeling, now that you mention it," confessed the Rat, puffing harder at his pipe so that its glow illuminated his face and eyes and showed how kindly he was looking upon his friend.

"Well then," said the Mole, "I would be regretful if I had not told you the gist of Badger's story as he told it me, and I do not think that he would mind at all – rather the opposite, in fact, for knowledge of it makes us understand a little better that wise animal's occasional moroseness, and also his compassion.

"I shall state the matter as simply as I can: those items you mention that I saw spoke not of Badger when he was young, as I first thought, but of the son he lost –"

"Badger had a son!" exclaimed the astonished Water Rat.

"We have no need to enquire into the details too much, but let me say that this is my understanding: Badger's father journeyed to the River Bank from western parts, across the wild and difficult country that lies there, and settled with his wife in the Wild Wood, whose dark dangers held no fears for him, and whose silent, awesome nature matched something in his own.

"In those days the weasels and the stoats were more fearsome than they are now and for many years Badger's father, and then Badger himself, fought to pacify and civilize the place. He kept himself to himself, and few along the River Bank ever saw him, and many did not even know that he existed.

"Of his meeting with that female whom he came to love I know nothing, but they had a family, all but one of whom, their son, perished in the Wild Wood, a noisome dank place surely not suited to the raising of a family. The boy's mother sought to persuade Badger to move on, asking him to travel up-river, just as we are doing, for she too had heard of Beyond and wanted to be nearer it in a more green and pleasant place, there to raise a second family.

"But Badger was stubborn and refused to move, saying that what was good enough for him should be good enough for his son. Be that as it may the boy's mother never got her way and, tragically, perished, as her other children had, in the dark depths of the Wild Wood, in circumstances – and Badger did not elaborate – that did no credit, none at all, to the reputation of the weasels and stoats.

"Badger has never forgiven himself for her death, or quite come to terms with the loss, and nor did his son. Eventually Badger's son matured, and decided to realize his mother's dream and journey up-river to find a better place, and put strife and sad memory behind him.

"Hard did the two badgers struggle over this, but in the end one left and one stayed. But the one who left was not heard of again, and though Badger mounted a search of a kind, he never found the truth of what had occurred."

"Did he find any clues, Mole?"

The Mole was silent for a long time.

"One alone," he said at last. "He learned that his son had reached a place called Lathbury, and he learned that he had been warned against continuing his journey. He learned that his son's stubbornness and determination had got the better of his prudence, and he had travelled on alone, never to be heard of more."

"The Lathbury Pike?" whispered the Rat.

"It may be so," said the Mole.

"And all these years –"

" – and all these years poor Badger has kept those

143

mementoes of his son in that spare room, and has lived alone with the regrets that come from losing the two he loved most of all and in such unhappy circumstances."

"But he could have tried to follow him —"

"He tried and it was too late. And yet —"

"Well, Mole?"

"Yet he said to me when we spoke of this that there are some nights when he stands on the bank somewhere between your home and Otter's, staring at the stars and rising moon, and he feels that the River seeks to tell him that somewhere beyond River Bank his son is still alive, and he too is standing on a river bank, wishing that the River could send a message of hope that one day, before Badger's last, that last argument would be undone, and a father and a son might be at peace with one another once again."

"Then —"

"Yes, Ratty, I think Badger hopes that in some way we can say a last goodbye for him, by journeying where he felt unable to, so that he might have a second chance through us."

Soon after this, and in a solemn frame of mind, for now they felt they were retracing the distant steps of one whom the Badger had once loved, the two companions found themselves in a wider, flatter area of open fields, and saw a small town ahead, and beyond it for the first time hills and distant mountains, and their hearts lifted, for here was evidence that the vision of Beyond they each had had in different ways was not so very far from the truth.

The furthest peaks they saw were too far off for an expedition such as theirs, but that rough forested ground they saw ahead might be within their reach, though taking their boats up might be difficult indeed.

"Forget the Pike," said the Rat; "just look at the gradient. It's going to be difficult, but we can only see how far we can get, eh Mole?"

"Come on," cried the Mole, much excited to have reached civilization once again. "Let's see if this is the Lathbury of which we've heard so much. Perhaps we can find that Tavern."

The River skirted the town in a wide meander, but such houses, gardens and roads as they could see seemed mostly uninhabited.

"It must be Sunday," said the Mole, putting the best complexion on things.

"Humph!" muttered the Rat, moving their weapons a little closer, for the more he looked at Lathbury the grubbier, the more unkempt, and the more run down it seemed. A place that time, and modernity, seemed to have quite passed by.

"Look! There's someone there," the Mole called out, pointing towards an old crumbling wall near the river bank.

But the person, darkly and closely dressed as if it was winter and not summer, simply stood and stared, and ignored their greetings. Then another peered at them round the corner of a house, and a third, pulling aside a curtain at a half-open cottage window, and not even answering their friendly wave.

They proceeded thus quite slowly, and made the firm

decision not to leave their boat and go exploring, for the locals seemed unfriendly if not yet quite hostile.

"Best to get through and beyond this place," said the Rat, "and find somewhere to camp for the night which we can defend easily. We had better be careful not to get split up, for there's safety in numbers when there's hostility about."

They had first sighted Lathbury in mid-afternoon, but so indirect was the meander, and so cautious was their passage that it was gone six o'clock before the River turned north away from what seemed the last house and they began to feel easy once again. Lathbury, or this side of it, did not seem to be a place to visit on a day such as this.

Soon they spied an old stone bridge, to the Lathbury side of which stood an old dwelling, dirty and ruinous, yet apparently occupied, from the sooty smoke that wound upwards from its chimneys. On drawing closer to it they saw it had a jetty along the river bank, and a peeling sign which read "THE HAT AND BOOT" and another reading "TRADITIONAL ALES AND SPIRITS". However, beneath these words was a less traditional greeting for weary travellers in need of board and lodging for the night: "*Boatmen and their dependants not welcome now or ever.*"

Nor was the inn sign quite traditional either, for it eschewed the bright warm colours of the kind in which sign painters normally depict their subjects to welcome potential customers. Instead, in medieval fashion, nailed upon the board which read The Hat and Boot was an ancient hat, and a bedraggled boot.

"We shall call in here and see what we can learn about

this Lathbury Pike," said the Rat, which is what the Mole feared he might say. If it had been up to him, the Mole would have given the evil-looking place a wide berth and proceeded on his way.

"I shall take my cudgel," said the Mole, "for I do not like the look of this hostelry one bit −"

"No need for that, Mole, we do not wish to cause offence, or provoke those who live here," said the Rat, before adding sensibly, "but we'll moor the boats on the far side of the bridge out of harm's way, where we can easily keep an eye on them, and get back to them in a hurry if we must."

The Tavern's old door creaked open at their push to reveal a small dark vestibule off which three doors led. Upon the one straight ahead was a notice written in a rough hand which read, "STRIKTLY PRIVATE, SO STAY OUT"; a second, to their left, had another notice which read "NOT THIS WAY"; so they took the third.

It opened onto a large stone-flagged room, dark and chillsome, in which a good many figures were gathered together, some morosely lounging against a long bar, tankard in hand, others huddled together on benches at rough tables, drinking beer and eating a mess of bread and pottage, and talking in low voices.

At their entrance all conversation ceased – and a silence fell upon the company as they turned and stared at the two intruders. They saw that each member of this unfriendly company was a very rough-looking representative of one of two species of animal that the Rat and the Mole did not much like: weasels and stoats. The weasels being, in the main, the solitary loungers; and the stoats, for the most part, the huddled eaters. Some were big, some small, some fat and some thin: not one displayed anything other than unpleasant curiosity.

"Food's off," growled a voice behind the bar, and they turned to see a tall cadaverous gentleman who was evidently the landlord.

"'Cept fer 'taters," screeched his wife's voice from somewhere upstairs and within. "So sell 'em yesterday's."

"Well –" began the Mole.

The landlord chose to take the Mole's hesitation for a firm order and, peering up some stairs, shouted, "Twice double portions, ducks."

Then he turned to them and put a restless hand upon a mahogany pump handle, not unlike a policeman's truncheon, and said, "Nah, fer drinks. Wot yer want?"

"I was thinking," said the Rat speaking as low as he could, for the silence of the Tavern had continued and all were listening to their every syllable, "of a traditional ale of the kind advertised outside."

"Were yer now?" said the landlord, studying them with seeming distaste.

"What kind of ale would that be?" persisted the Rat.

"There's three," said the landlord, "and they're all brewed on the premises. There's Policeman's Punch, if yer wanna few. There's Bishop's Blasphemy, if yer like that kind of thing. And the strongest we got is Judge and Jury, but more 'n a pint and yer'll need help getting home."

"Well then," said the Rat, anxious to get the transaction over as quickly as possible, "we'll have a pint each of Policeman's Punch."

They took their brimming tankards to a table where three stoats reluctantly made room for them, and in a few moments a plate of potatoes each was duly served. Interest in the strangers began to wane and conversation to resume.

"How much will that be?" asked the Mole, for the landlord was hovering.

"Depends if yer comin' or goin'," he replied.

"I am not sure I understand," said the Rat.

"Seems plain enough to me," said the landlord. "Comin' is downaways and goin' is upaways."

"You mean down-river or up-river."

"That's what 'e said," said a stoat sitting near them.

"And there's a difference in price, is there?" said the Mole, sensing some more duping on the way.

"If yer comin', which means yer goin' back into Lathbury Town, that'll be tuppence three farthings each for the 'taters, and a penny a pint for the beer, or give us 'alf a crahn and call it quits."

The stoats winked at each other, and another general silence fell to see if the visitors would yield to this extortion or argue the point.

"And if we're going on upstream?" said the Rat.

"If yer were, which yer'd be advised not to, then by rights yer get as much of the Blasphemy as yer can drink at one go free, and a 'elpin' more of the tatties to take with yer."

"Free?" said the Mole.

"Yeh, but yer not."

"But we are," said the Mole very firmly. "We *are* journeying up-river. That's what you call 'going', isn't it?"

For the first time in their conversation the landlord appeared lost for words, and the room fell into a deeper silence, but one now more curious and astonished than hostile.

"Well, I wouldn't."

"But we shall," said the Rat, "so charge us a fair price for the food and drink and we'll be on our way."

"Well, yer mad. The food and drinks are free, but I'll charge yer two groat for the conversation."

This the Rat duly paid and honour seemed satisfied all round. The potatoes were good, but the beer was lethal, so they only sipped at it.

"Yer not really goin' upstream, are yer?" said one of the stoats with a good deal more respect in his voice than before.

"We are," said the Mole firmly. "Is there a reason why not?"

The stoats laughed, and soon the whole room joined in. But when they saw that the Mole and the Rat did not laugh and were quite serious in their intent, one of the stoats said, "Don't yer know, mate?"

"Know what?"

"The reason yer shouldn't be goin' upstream is the Pike, the Lathbury Pike."

"What of it?" said the Mole boldly. In such circumstances the Rat could not but admire his normally timid friend for his bold front.

"Don't tell us yer not heard of it?"

"We have heard but little of it down our way," said the Rat carefully. "Perhaps you could tell us more?"

The stoat needed no second invitation and, egged on by his friends who crowded round, and a few of the weasels who came over and joined them, he gave a detailed and bloody account of the Pike's ferocity (it thought nothing of sinking boats) and diet (it especially liked babies, young lambs and piglets if it could get them).

"Once upon a time the farmers of the pastures up top – that was afore the 'igh Judge acquired the land and turned 'em off for good – walked their cattle across the River upstream to get to Lathbury market quicker, but that were no good, no good at all. Too many taken, you see?"

"Whole cows eaten by the Pike?" exclaimed the Mole.

"Two at a time when she were nurturing a brood," said one of the weasels almost cheerfully. "That's why they built the bridge, 'cos farmers wouldn't risk it by river no more. No farmers now, any road."

"Has anyone ever *seen* the Pike?" asked the Rat, dubious about these claims.

"She's too cunning and too quick to be seen, but for the vast shadow of 'er across the pool, but they've 'eard 'er many a time and seen sign of 'er."

"Heard her?" said the Mole, his eyes wide. "Seen signs?"

"Aye, 'eard 'er wooshing in the water at dusk, when they say she exercises 'er tail so's she can swim faster, and that sets up the waves they seen."

"So what do river travellers do if they want to go past where the Lathbury Pike lives?" asked the Rat, reasonably enough.

"Not many wants to go on up there," said their informant darkly. "No roads up there now worth the name, and no one in their right minds living there neither. They'm lost souls live up there now, driven daft by the Pike, don't you see? If you've a mind to go on then the only thing to do is to 'ave your craft taken out of the River downstream and transported by road, especially in the months o' June and July."

"You mean *now*?" said the Mole.

The stoat nodded slowly, eyes narrowing, seeming almost to revel in his tale.

"Bred by now; be raising a brood by now."

"Hasn't anyone ever tried to kill the Lathbury Pike?" said the Rat stoutly. "Anyway, she must be very old by now."

"O, don't make that mistake, sir," (they were beginning

to treat the Mole and the Rat with considerable respect by now) "really you mun't. Many's said the same and after a few years of quiet they've taken their boats up the creek where she lives and all that's ever seen of them again is their boats, and their 'ats and boots. She don't eat 'ats and she don't eat boots."

"Aye," said the landlord, putting in his pennyworth, "why do you think it's called the Hat and Boot Tavern?"

"Surely not – ?" began the Mole, now seriously concerned.

"It's surely so," said another. "Off they go out of this door, their bellies full of free drink –"

"Why do you serve it free?" said the Rat, interrupting.

"Ancient statute," said the landlord. "In the old days it gave young bloods the courage to go and kill the Pike, but we live in modern times now, eh lads?"

"That's right!"

"But we keeps up the tradition."

"And the hat and boot that's hanging up outside now," asked the Mole; "that's just for show, isn't it?"

"That's no show," said the landlord. "Old Tom'll tell you 'cos 'e was 'ere when the last damn fool – beggin' yer pardon, gents – went up-river."

"Aye," said Tom, who came over and joined them, "it was a cold and chilly night when 'e come, and I remember it like it was –"

"Make it snappy, Tom, don't give 'em the whole works; they'll be dead in their seats afore you finish."

"It was a badger," said the landlord, "a very big badger, weren't it, Tom?"

"Aye, so it was, fine and young he was. That was afore

you came, afore many of the lads 'ere was even born. Came here and sat right where you're sittin' now, sir," he said, pointing at the Rat's seat.

The Water Rat felt very uncomfortable at this and shifted slightly in his seat.

"'E was warned, but he weren't listening, like badgers often don't. He upped and went and three days later down they came – 'is hat and boot. That was all was left, yer see. So we 'ung 'em up out of respect, and as a warning."

"So now you know," said the landlord; "and that's why I say yer won't be going –"

"O, but we are," said the Mole, standing up with sudden resolution, "and right now! Come on, Ratty, we'll not listen to any more of this talk or we'll never get going!"

The landlord and his clients followed them out, tankards in hand, blinking in the bright sunshine and chattering like women at a public execution. There were last-minute directions and advice, and a few final warnings and appeals against their journey before the Rat told the Mole to cast off the painter.

The Tavern, and its clients, slowly disappeared downstream behind them.

·VIII·
In Pursuit of Love

Toad's journey up-river towards the Town had a very different flavour from when the Rat and the Mole had taken the same route some weeks before, as different as chalk and cheese.

They had gone slowly and gently, in harmony with nature generally, and the River in particular, their spirits and their days attuned to the rising of the dawn and the setting of the sun. For them it was the simple pleasures that mattered – listening to the lapping of the water along the banks, enjoying the rustle of the summer breeze through rush and sedge, and the shimmering of birch leaves in the wind across the fields. If a mallard led a squeaking busy brood across their path, the Rat and the Mole paused to let them safely by; if a pair of swans glided upstream of them and silently turned and drifted sideways to the current, they stopped awhile to admire the grand spectacle.

But then came Toad, and not for him such sentimental nonsense!

The rustling breeze?

Toad could not hear it at all because of the noise his loud and shuddering engine made.

The shimmering birch leaves?

Toad could not see any trees and leaves because of the spray the bows of his racing launch threw up.

Dabbling ducks?

"Out of my way!" cried Toad.

Elegant swans?

"Horrid things, stop hogging the River!" yelled Toad.

The roar of his craft, the thwack! thwack! of its prow as it hit the water, and not least the sight of Toad himself, steering with one hand and gesticulating with the other that all other users of the River, be they flesh, fish or fowl, get out of his way, caused a general evacuation of all living things along his route.

Cows and sheep turned and fled across fields at his loud approach; horses bolted in alarm, leaping gates to get away; rooks flocked up from trees and headed to all points of the compass in their eagerness to escape. As for those fish unfortunate enough to be harmlessly grubbing about amongst the weed and mud beneath the water, such as roach and perch, silver dace and stickleback, the shock of Toad's passage caused general panic and disarray.

While those skulking creatures, the treacherous and cowardly weasels and stoats, hid from him as he sped by and for half an hour afterwards.

Naturally Toad was oblivious of all this and the effect he was having on those about him, just as he always had been. In any case, he had more important things to think about, for his motor-launch offered challenges he had not met and conquered before.

At first he could not quite master the art of steering around bends, and would weave desperately from one side of the River to the other, scattering mud and broken vegetation in his efforts to avoid its banks. Twice he failed in this endeavour and the craft was brought to a grinding halt prow-first in the gravel and mud of the bank. It would have been better for all concerned if matters had ended there and then. But so powerful were the engines of the launch, so easy and effective its reverse controls, and so determined was the lovelorn swain to catch up with his lady love once more, that he did not let these mishaps delay him long. Toad was an enthusiastic if impatient learner.

Before long he had worked out how to speed up, accelerating as he approached each new bend in the meandering River and shouting "Wheee!" as he went round it, and "Whooo!" as he drew out of it and took up a straighter course once more.

This soon bored him and he began to explore the higher speeds of his excellent craft, with utter disregard for frantic wildfowl, and the effect of the wash and the waves upon the banks. But this too became tedious and repetitive and he tried slowing down and then surging suddenly forward in a most wilful way. But even that was not much fun after a while.

Toad became ever more adventurous as he successively tried steering with one hand and his eyes shut, then standing on one leg and merely caressing the wheel with a finger or two; then, ever more balletic, Toad tried letting go and describing the odd pirouette about the deck before taking up the wheel once more –

"Vroom! Vroom!" he cried.

Then, standing upon the higher deck and hooking one foot upon the wheel, both to steer and hold him in at the same time, the foolish Toad leaned out across the water, which raced past beneath him – "Vroom! Wheee! Whoosh!"

It would be good and just to be able to report that Toad came a cropper; very satisfactory to report that Toad crashed the offending craft irrecoverably; just and equitable to be able to say that Toad fell in and got very wet and muddy and was forced to limp the long way home, a wiser and more reasonable animal.

But Fate is fickle and unjust, and sometimes smiles upon those whom ordinary, sober, hard-working mortals rightly condemn. Indeed, Fate sometimes goes out of its way to help the Toads of this world and heap upon them the fortune and riches that its favours bring.

So it was that afternoon with Toad. Whatever he did in that lunatic voyage in pursuit of the Madame, whether it was controlling the boat with only one foot on the wheel, or doing a quick hand-stand or two, or putting the craft into full throttle while he just popped below decks to see what victuals and beverages the excellent Prendergast had laid in store, inflicted no setback at all: the odd bump, the odd brief grounding, but nothing, absolutely nothing, seriously delayed his progress.

Finally, as the afternoon light began to wane, Toad, by now going more slowly and calmly, and with a Havana in his left hand and a brimming glass of champagne adjacent to the other, saw ahead of him His Lordship's House. He did not immediately recognize it since the last time he had come that way was from the air, drifting down in a parachute. But once he drew closer he saw that same hot-house roof with which he had once had an uncomfortable acquaintance.

"Ha, ha!" said he, chortling to himself, "I have arrived unnoticed and will now proceed with caution. The Madame's hand will not be won by foolhardy bravado but by a cunning strategy that combines stealth and resolution, with a clear plan and rapid execution. I shall rescue her from the unwelcome attentions of the High Judge, we shall escape in my waiting craft, and then –"

But Toad, as is the way with lovers, was not much concerned with what happened afterwards. Jealousy was his motivation, re-possession his present goal.

He perused the chart and saw that the small tributary he had espied just before he reached His Lordship's estate was clearly marked, with some useful tips for mariners: *"Dangerous channel; not navigable; underwater obstructions; subject to the laws of statutory trespass and instant trial before the Admiralty Offences Board; therefore River-users strongly advised to avoid."*

"Ideal," said Toad, chuckling at his quick-thinking cleverness and bravado, "I shall moor the craft down there, for no one will think to search for it in so inhospitable a place."

He turned sharply about, shot back down river, saw that same barbed wire and notice with which the Mole had tangled some days before, and powered his craft straight through the lot of it, coming to rest safely and out of view among the high reeds upon His Lordship's bank. There he made the boat fast, and climbed out onto dry land once more.

"My sweet, my dear," he announced to the nearest tree stump, by way of practice and to work up his passion once again, "I am coming to you now! Can you sense the imminence of my arrival? Do your instincts tell you that your Toad is near? I shall find thee a gift, a bouquet perhaps —"

But a search amongst the bank-side vegetation yielded nothing more than some of last year's bulrushes, the poor frail blooms of eglantine, and some yellow flag which cut his hands when he tried to pick it. A rustic lover might have made much even of this limited fare, but one such as Toad, spoilt by a lifetime of self-indulgence, gave up the endeavour on the instant and decided to entrust the finding of a floral gift to Providence, which had served him so well for so long, and might be expected to turn up trumps on his behalf a few times more.

Meanwhile he swiftly penned a proposal of marriage to his beloved on a page torn from his craft's log, in case there were too little time for words, in which he promised her his eternal fidelity and love, and all his worldly goods. Then he set off to find her, with Providence firmly on his side.

For one thing, His Lordship's hounds had been locked up early in their kennels for the day, from where they were able only to bay and bark harmlessly at his furtive presence as he advanced through shrubberies and vegetable gardens and then across the lawns.

Then Providence smiled yet more sweetly upon Toad, for it guided him towards the house by way of a large yew hedge and then along a brick path which passed one end of that hothouse whose roof, and prickly plants, he remembered so well.

It was a warm evening and the air was heavy with the musky scents of the blooms within, a few of which he could vaguely make out through moist and misted glass. Even though the light was beginning to fail, the brilliant reds and yellows of their petals, the voluptuous purples and sensuous apricots of their stamens and pistils all revealed themselves when he peered in.

Once this floral extravaganza had been seen and scented by Toad, he could not resist the temptation offered him to create a bouquet of bouquets, and one that would surely win the heart of the Madame. How could a lady, however hard-hearted she seemed, resist a billet doux of the kind he had so passionately penned when accompanied by a bouquet of blooms so exotic and expressive?

He tried a door, it opened, and in he hurried to help himself, as thoughtlessly as he had always helped himself to the good things of life – and not bothering to read the notices there prominently displayed over every door and bay: SEVERE AND EXTREME PENALTY FOR TOUCHING, HARMING OR PICKING ANY OF THE COLLECTION'S FLORA *by Order of the High Judge.*

It must not be thought that Toad did not appreciate the blooms he had discovered, for he did. He sniffed at them heartily, as he might at a joint of well-cooked beef, he exclaimed his pleasure cheerfully, and he declared rather too loudly, "Flowers fit for a queen!"

Toad then danced about, helping himself with that same gay and self-satisfied abandon with which he had earlier that day guided his launch upstream. With a quick pick here and a hard pull there he set to work gathering the brightest, largest and most scented blooms in an impulsive and carefree manner that led him up and down the aisles of His Lordship's hothouse, and left behind him a trail of floral ruin and arboreal destruction.

Thus satisfied, and now humming happily to himself as

swains will who have at last found a satisfactory gift for their beloved, Toad sought to retrace his steps to the door by which he had entered, but he could not immediately find it. In so large and grand a hothouse one aisle is much like another, one row of plants no different from the next, especially when many of their best blooms have been removed and they have been reduced to bare and boring foliage, and so Toad began to wander about seeking an exit.

It was as he was thus employed that he turned a corner and found himself approaching a pair of French doors through whose glass he could see a well-lit morning room of some kind, all gilt and mirrors and marble statues, but with little furniture.

In the middle of this room Toad saw a grouping of three gentlemen, all past their best years, arranged upon a dais in poses rather less ebullient than that triumphal one Toad himself had essayed some weeks before.

One, whose face Toad knew to be that of the High Judge himself, sat in a simple oak chair and had about him the look of Justice.

The second gentleman, whom Toad was uncomfortably aware of having seen before, though not wearing the linen sheet which was now draped about his puny torso, represented Law.

"O dear!" muttered Toad unhappily to himself, clutching his stolen bouquet all the tighter. "Here is not just the High Judge, but the Commissioner of Police as well!"

Then, moving rapidly on to the third figure he asked himself, "Could this be − ?"

He looked, and knew immediately that it was just as he feared: he was fast approaching the three people he least wished to meet in the whole world, especially in combination. For the last gentleman stood behind the other two, holding a crook in his hand – the very representation of the Established Church.

"It's that same Lord Bishop I met in the hothouse last time I dropped in," said Toad, trying to put as positive a complexion on that doleful incident as he could.

There were two more figures in the room, though for the moment he had eyes only for one of them. For there, her words muted by the glass of the French doors, but her gestures and stance as loud and raucous as ever, was his cousin Madame d'Albert, caught in the very act of pushing, prodding and persuading her subjects into a pose which she intended to sketch and afterwards re-form into a sculptural group.

The other person in the room –

But before Toad could take in what he saw, he was accosted by an infirm gentleman holding a rake.

This was the Head Gardener (retired) who, up till that moment, had given over sixty years of unimpeachable service to His Lordship, his Lordship's father, and *his* father before that, having started in the vegetable garden at the age of twelve.

O fickle Fate, that smiles so illiberally upon a villain such as Toad, yet turns her back upon a deserving old gentleman now nearly infirm, and (as it happened) but two days from final and complete retirement. Forty-eight hours more, and that good, kind gentleman might have lived his remaining years in bliss, and his twelve children and thirty-six grandchildren with their family reputation pure as unsullied snow.

But it was not to be.

"My man," said Toad loftily, "give me that rake at once and get out of my way, for I have work to do!"

Work!

Had not the speechless gardener worked? Had he not tended the *Orchis celebrata* whose solitary bloom, nine years in the growing, Toad now so rudely held?

Work!? Had he not nurtured that *Acer himalaya* that his High Lordship himself had collected on his Nepalese journey in '89, and which had finally succeeded in seeding only a week before?

Work?!!!?

Had not his gnarled and arthritic hands –

The old Head Gardener was able to say nothing as these thoughts raged through his dumb-founded brain, so shocked and appalled was he, and he allowed Toad to take the rake from his shaking hands without resistance of any kind; but he did not get out of the way quite swiftly enough.

True love certainly does not run smooth, especially for those who get in its way.

"Stop dawdling, and pot a few more plants if you have nothing better to do!" cried the heartless Toad, pushing the old man into the nearest flower bed and advancing past him with a look of determination on his face.

Certainly Toad had something more important than a doddery gardener upon his mind, and it concerned that last person he had espied in the morning room, and at whom he now stared unseen, a look of fury, rage and jealousy suffusing his face. For there, quite open and brazen, was the person the Madame had referred to before she had fled Toad Hall, the person who stood between Toad and his beloved.

Toad had been quite prepared to fight for her hand against judges, policemen and bishops, all together if need be, but he had not expected his rival to be younger than he, and a toad as well! He had certainly not expected him to be attired in the silks, ruffles and feathers of a louche fop, and to have about his waist a jewelled belt from which hung a scabbard in which seemed to be a real sword; and on his head a huge felt hat of the type that Gallic musketeers, and Romeos, are inclined to wear when they go about their professional business.

In normal times Toad might have decided that in all the circumstances, with the forces of Law, Order and the Church arrayed against him, and a rival who seemed his match as well, it might have been best to let discretion be the better part of valour, and beat a hasty retreat before he was seen. But jealousy is indiscreet, love unmanageable, and Toad's blood was up.

He eyed the bejewelled sword once more, saw the slim and elegant toad who wore it bow low before the Madame and kiss her hand – a kiss Toad would have been happier to see her reject with a disgusted look upon her face – and Toad followed the jealous longings and inclinations of his heart.

Pushing the French doors open and stepping inside, he paused long enough for all parties therein to see him, before brandishing the rake above his head and declaiming in a loud voice, "This is my trusty sword and with it

I shall cut down and destroy my enemies and all those who insult the one I love!"

Then, advancing upon the villain who fondled the Madame's hand, he said, "Unhand her, villain, and defend yourself!"

His cry, his wild and dangerous gestures, and this final challenge appeared so to surprise and unnerve those upon whom he advanced that for a moment or two they stood stock still, as in some medieval tableau, caught forever in an act that future generations might find very mysterious indeed.

But Toad was not so stilled, and his mind felt as sharp as if it had recently been honed upon a barber's strop. Seeing his moment of advantage, he advanced a few paces, pushed aside his rival, went down upon one knee and, presenting his bouquet and accompanying letter to the Madame, made this pretty speech: "Madame, accept this missive as my proposal of marriage, and these paltry blooms as an emblem of my sentiments. Pray, choose one that I may carry it upon my person as your favour in that battle in which I must now engage as your knight to protect the honour I have here seen stained and spoiled by this rogue!"

Closer examination of the rogue showed him to be even younger in years than Toad had at first thought him. Indeed he was barely out of childhood, and someone with more experience of youthful play would have realized at once that the youth was in some form of fancy dress and certainly not the brazen cad Toad had thought him to be. Indeed, putting two and two together, almost anyone other than Toad would have deduced that the "villain" he now proposed to assassinate was the Madame's young son, he to whom, as she had told Toad before, her whole life was dedicated.

But Toad was not now to be stopped, and had already raised his rake in what he imagined to be the correct position for one embarking upon a fencing duel with a rival. A proceeding that might not have mattered too much had not the youth – who, even more than Toad, had the air of one used to having his own way, spoilt and indulged from the first moments of his birth – had not this youth, thinking Toad to be some hireling actor or tomfool brought in for the occasion for his personal entertainment, decided that it would be amusing to take the challenge seriously.

"En garde!" said he, drawing his sword and taking up a position opposite Toad.

The sight of the sword sharp and glittering before his nose and the fierce determination of the unpleasant youth rather surprised Toad, who so far as he had thought about the business at all, had assumed that any rival he might have would instantly flee before his challenge.

Quite plainly this was not to be, just as it was plain that Toad had challenged a mere whippersnapper who might have been better dealt with by being led out of the room by the scruff of the collar.

"En garde!" the youth cried again. "You insult *Maman* with your attention not-wanted, and for that I will kill you!"

Toad decided that the best approach was to bluff it out and, still feeling that etiquette demanded that he attempt to wield his rake like a duelling sword, he made a few passes in the air, cut a few bold swathes and advanced upon the boy, crying, "Yield now and your honour will be saved!"

The three elderly eminences seemed as struck dumb by Toad's antics as the Head Gardener had been, but the Madame very quickly recovered her composure.

"Monsieur Toad!" she cried, seeking to intervene in a duel which, knowing the participants as she did, she guessed would come to no good. "I am pleased to introduce you to my son the Count d'Albert-Chapelle."

"Ha!" cried the youth, ignoring his mother completely (as he had done since a babe) and counter-attacking Toad with such speed, grace and ruthlessness that it was painfully clear which of the two contestants had had lessons in swordcraft in a Parisian gymnasium, and which had not.

"And my dear son, *mon petit chou*," continued the Madame, "I am so very glad that you now 'ave the opportunity to play with your English uncle. But now this silly game must STOP!"

"Bah!" grunted Toad, irritated at being forced into retreat and feeling it would do his cause no good to suffer defeat at the hands of a mere youth. With an astonishing speed for one so rotund, and with an impressive sweep and cut of the rake he attempted to finish off the youth with one mighty blow, hoping to sort out the matter with his mother afterwards.

The boy leapt back with agility, deflected Toad's new attack, and caused the rake to descend upon the feet, and more particularly the toes, of the High Judge, the Commissioner of Police and the Bishop all at once. This woke them from the slumber of surprise and shock into which they seemed to have fallen and with one voice they began shouting accusations and threats, while at the same time summoning the various servants, police constables, chaplains, clerks of the court and all the other hangers-on which great and important men have nearby wherever they go, awaiting their beck and call.

It would be impossible to describe in any detail the confusion of the following moments. But as Toad began

to retreat before his skilled adversary once more, their battleground, the morning room, began to fill up with an increasingly large number of men, some in blue uniforms, some in black robes, and not a few wearing clerical outfits. All were eager to help, and to be seen to help. They needed only the clear command of the superior who had summoned them to know what they must do.

The Commissioner of Police was quite sure that the law was being broken, if only on the grounds of the peace being disturbed, and that arrests should be made by his officers there and then, and he cried, "Arrest him!"

Twelve constables then attempted to do so.

The High Judge was certain that a large number of crimes were being committed before his very eyes, including trespass (of his property and person), felony, larceny and burglary (of his specimen plants and garden implements), assault and battery *and* probably grievous bodily harm *and* attempted murder (upon Madame's son) and a variety of additional crimes he was pondering upon. So he cried, "Try him!"

Six clerks of court proceeded towards the preparation of the paperwork by asking the suspect his full name, address and date of birth.

The Senior Bishop saw a tormented soul upon the slippery slopes of spiritual decline who might still be drawn back into the family of the Church, given sufficient help and guidance. He therefore cried out, "Save him!"

And a Deacon Parishionary, a Dean-in-Ordinary, and an Acting Bishop Extraordinary, each brandishing various gospels, crosses and crosiers, rushed towards him who needed immediate spiritual help and sustenance.

O fickle fickle Fate, which makes such a mockery of Man's best intentions, and leads the forces of the Law and Justice and the Church so far astray.

For though they all rushed forward to do their duty, it was towards the wrong toad. Mischievous and wicked Fate did not guide them towards Toad of Toad Hall, for he wielded merely a rake, and seemed, so far as they could judge, to be defending himself and a female personage against a trained and murderous swordsman.

It was upon the callow Count d'Albert-Chapelle they charged, to arrest, arraign and save his soul. It was he whose sword was torn from his grasp and sent skittering across the floor; he whose hat was trampled upon and whose silken garb was torn; and he who protested loudly in a foreign tongue, thereby compounding his obvious guilt (and need of saving) a hundredfold with each foreign word that was uttered.

While Toad of Toad Hall, astonished, found himself sitting upon the floor by the side of his cousin, some way from the *mêlée*, unmolested and unnoticed.

A variety of thoughts went through his mind, the chief one being that if he were to escape with his life, now was the moment to do it; to which was added the idea that he might as well escape with the one he loved and leave the insolent son to his fate.

Far, far behind these thoughts was a vague disquiet at seeing his rival so brutally suppressed, handcuffed and arraigned, and asked by various prelates whether or not he had any last words, and if he had would he be good enough to speak them in the mother tongue, which is to say English.

Toad was about to rise, offer himself once more to the Madame, allay any doubts she might have about leaving her son behind and suggest they flee His Lordship's House *immédiatement.*

But the lady spoke first.

"Mon dieu!" cried she. "Cousin, save 'im from these devils! 'E is my son! 'E has never been good, never do what I say, but 'e 'as not been so bad as this!"

Toad rose and stared across the room at where the youth struggled still and those words she spoke "he has not been as bad as this" struck a chord deep within his heart, very deep indeed. And now that her son's sword had been taken from him, and his hat removed, and his clothes half torn off he was but a sorry and pathetic sight, and Toad saw that the look of spoilt petulance had gone, gone completely, as had the smugness he had displayed but minutes before when he had been about to humiliate Toad with his superior swordplay.

Instead he saw a very frightened young toad, and one who could not quite understand how a bit of fun, harmless as it had seemed, had brought upon him the wrath of so many men in uniforms whose sole intention was to take all the fun away, and replace it with the misery of deprivation and incarceration.

"He has not been as bad as this," she had said, and Toad could not but think how often, how very often, such a thing might have been said about himself and his own harmless deeds; and how, when Fate was not upon his side, his friends along the River Bank often were, and came quickly to his aid.

Toad stared aghast at the defeated and now helpless,

hopeless, friendless youth, and saw himself when young, and remembered how rare it was that help came when it was needed, and how infrequently the true cause of Justice and of Law was served in so punishing him.

"Cousin –" Madame began again, but she had no need to plead.

Toad rose as if in a dream, and a chord louder than love rang in his heart, and one that drove off fear.

Taking up the sword that had fallen on the floor, and feeling perhaps that what the outnumbered French youth needed was the sound of his own language, he cried the inspiring words of the new-found selfless revolutionary, *"Liberté! Egalité! Fraternité!"*, and charged to rescue his former foe.

If words failed earlier to describe the arrival of the constables, clerks and clerics, they utterly do so now to give any adequate account of the confusion of the retreat of these henchmen before Toad's might and ire.

It was enough to see the look in his eyes, and to see the purposeful strength with which he wielded the sword, to be still; it was enough to hear his raging commands to yield, to let the lad go, his handcuffs quickly undone.

"Madame!" cried Toad, her son now propped half fainting in his left arm and the sword raised still in his right hand. "You shall not suffer punishment, for you have done no wrong. Therefore it is safe to leave you behind for the moment. But we, that is your son here the Count and I, Toad of Toad Hall, who both hold you in love and esteem, are fugitives from justice now. Love has caused us to break the paltry laws of the state; may love support us through the long years of flight that must lie ahead!"

Such was Toad's final speech before he turned back to the French doors into the hothouse, pulling the youth bodily after him, and pushed the Head Gardener (retired) back once more into the flower bed from which he had been struggling so hard to emerge.

Then, with a laugh both light and cavalier, Toad thrust the sword through the handles of the doors to prevent them being opened, and was gone, leaving behind him a room of silent, wondering men.

And a single woman too. One who with Toad's rescue of her errant son, and with Toad's heroic speech, had seen at last the one for whom she would willingly move the very earth; and upon whom she would now bestow the passion and the favour of her heart.

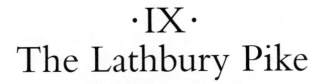

·IX·
The Lathbury Pike

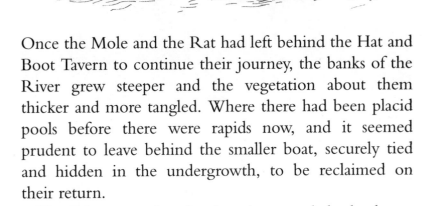

Once the Mole and the Rat had left behind the Hat and
Boot Tavern to continue their journey, the banks of the
River grew steeper and the vegetation about them
thicker and more tangled. Where there had been placid
pools before there were rapids now, and it seemed
prudent to leave behind the smaller boat, securely tied
and hidden in the undergrowth, to be reclaimed on
their return.

The River roared so loud at times, and the banks on
either side loomed so high, that the brightest part of the
day seemed dark, and they often had to communicate

with shouts and gestures. The further they went the more gorge-like the route became, and in places they had to drag the boat through the water with ropes about their chests, for punting or rowing was not always possible.

"A few more days, Mole, and we'll have to think of turning back," said the Rat.

But peering up the course of the roaring River, through the overhanging trees, they occasionally caught glimpses of huge skies and distant hills and mountains, and these intrigued the Mole.

"I just want to get beyond that rise of ground, even if we must leave the boat and walk the last part," he explained. "If only we can catch a glimpse of that mysterious place beyond all this, and also prove there's no great Pike here that travellers should worry about! Perhaps one day in the future my brave Nephew will come this way and take up the journey where we must soon leave it −"

A rush of wind, an extra roar of water.

"I can't hear you, Mole, old fellow; the River's roar is too loud," shouted the Rat. "Let's go on a bit, for it's too cold here to hang about."

"What I said can wait," the Mole shouted back; "so let's get on!"

On the third day after this, or perhaps the fourth or fifth − for time in that strange enshadowed place seemed to pass according to its own strange rules − the River widened into a run of deep, peat-stained pools. The banks were steep now, and very high, and the ground beyond so treacherous with the tangle of wet roots and moss, loose rocks and great impenetrable ferns that the only way forward was by water.

They had to stop sometimes to rest and eat, but all they could do was tie their painter to an overhanging root and dig their oars hard into what mud and grit there was to keep the boat steady. But the constant unremitting roar of water made them uneasy, and they fancied the trees had eyes and the wet vegetation about them hid the faces of enemies who spied on them and wished them ill.

In one such place they succeeded in clambering up the rocky banks and exploring a little, but when they returned to their craft they found the wet ground bore the unmistakable footprints of other creatures.

"Humph!" declared the Rat, gripping the cutlass he now habitually carried and staring into the shadows to make sure they were not about to be ambushed. "These are big fellows who have been here."

"Not just mere weasels and stoats, that's certain," said the Mole, "but they do not seem to have interfered with our boat or the gear in it. They could have caused us a good deal of inconvenience if they had."

The Water Rat glowered, annoyed with himself for taking such a risk, for he knew what a parlous position they would have been in had the person or persons who had spied on them – and might be spying still – untied their craft and let it drift out into the dangerous waters. The regulars at the Tavern far downstream would have had rather more than hats and boots to gossip about.

Chastened by this experience and resolved not to leave the boat unattended again, they set off once more.

"We must be careful, Mole, for this is no place to capsize or tumble in. The currents are swift and it would be too dangerous to try to turn back to rescue someone. Are you quite sure you're game to carry on?"

The water ran wide and deep now, and far ahead they saw a waterfall, above and beyond which was that alluring mountainous prospect they had seen earlier, and the drift of huge birds circling black against the sky.

"As far as the waterfall," said the Mole; "that's our destination, for we can take the boat no further. If we can climb up to the plateau above, well and good, but if not I shall be well satisfied. And we'll have proved there's no such thing as the Lathbury Pike!"

They decided to try to rest well that last night of their outward journey, satisfied with what they had done, though disappointed they had not done more; and tired, very tired, for the last days had been almost too much, and so noisy an animal could hardly think straight . . .

The Mole woke with a start in the night to the sound of his dreams and nightmares of a Pike and its brood, rapine and dangerous; and the whoosh! whoosh! whoosh! of its tail in the dark.

"What's that, Ratty?" said he fearfully.

"Nothing, Mole, nothing. Just the roar of the River torrents in the night."

Morning came at last, and with it the blessed relief of sunshine. The pools of the River ahead sparkled as the Rat rowed well and cheerfully, for they had been heartened to see a craft moored up near the waterfall – an old punt of rude but sturdy design – which suggested somebody must be about.

"Not far now, Ratty," said the Mole, for the air was growing damp with the mist from the waterfall.

"Go back! *You two!* Go back this instant!"

The warning seemed to come from the shadows surrounding the great deep pool, and as the Rat stopped sculling and held the boat steady they searched to see who called.

"Turn and go back, for the Pike breeds here! Go back! No one wants you here. Go!"

Then the Mole saw him, standing on a rock steadying himself with a stave: a badger huge and dark, shaking a fist at them. And he wore sturdy boots of the kind that might very well have left the marks they had seen upon the bank.

"Ratty, he's over there, just *there*, can't you see?"

Perhaps in the moment the Rat turned to look he loosened his grip on one of the oars, or perhaps the thumping jolt of the underwater obstruction that seemed to catch the boat at that same instant was so powerful he could never have held her steady anyway.

But even as the badger gave another warning shout, the water on their right side heaved darkly, and something golden-dark and huge surged and turned, and they saw eyes as evil and yellow as bile, with scales as ruddy red as the setting sun, and the boat rocked and heaved uncontrollably till it was suddenly turned over by the power of the beast that sought to take them.

"Ratty, help!"

"Mole, I can't – !"

All then was raging water, and surf, and the boil of river depths filled with the race of bubbles, and the tangle of gear and rope, and loose oars, and a creature that seemed more huge and terrible than anything they had ever known.

"Ratty!" cried the Mole, reaching out to his friend with one hand while clinging on with the other to his cudgel. "Ratty – !"

But it was no good, for poor Ratty, always the strongest swimmer, Ratty the friend who always found a solution to their problems – Ratty was torn by the beast from the Mole's weakening grasp in a boiling, raging, swirling whoosh of water and cruel teeth, and then gone from sight at the murderous beat of a massive tail.

Somehow or other the Mole clambered then to the shore, his club still in his hand, dazed and shaking with cold and fear. The place was dark and shadowed by great and ancient trees, the rocks covered in ferns and wet moss, and for a moment the Mole turned instinctively to try to climb up to dry land and out of harm's way.

Then he heard a cry, turned back towards the torrent and saw a heave of water, the slow rise of that great tail, and in the Pike's fearful mouth the colour of a jacket he knew too well.

Mole of Mole End of the River Bank, the one whom Nephew believed to be the greatest Mole who ever lived, knew no fear then. That Mole was suddenly courage personified.

Back into the water he stormed, wading, swimming, pulling himself to where the Rat and the Pike struggled, flailing with his cudgel at the great vile thing, and continuing even after it finally let go the Rat's spent form and turned upon him.

"Ratty, I'll never – !"

But then the Mole knew no more.

He felt a sharp tearing at the lower half of his body, a searing pain, and knew the terror of descending into the enfolding darkness of deep ice-cold water, and the fading of the light, and air, and life far far above his head and beyond his reach.

All was darkness and silence.

The Mole woke to the bliss of a warm, lavender-scented bed in which he seemed to float in endless comfort, drifting from day to night, from night to day.

"Sir! Please, sir, can you hear me now? Try to wake up –"

A voice, which though deep was young, though gruff was kind and much concerned.

"I'm Mole," he whispered, very happily, for to say his name was to say he was alive, "of Mole End –" and he drifted back to a healing sleep that had seemed to start long long before, in a place far far away.

Only slowly, as the days passed by, did wakefulness begin to come more often, and he accepted with gratitude the kind help of the young badger in whose home he was recovering. He accepted the water he was helped to drink, and the herbal teas as well; and finally the wholesome soups and nutty bread whose crumbs fell onto his chin and into his bed from where his helper removed them.

Only slowly, and most reluctantly, did he begin to remember what had happened, and to accept the fact that poor Ratty, his dearest closest friend was surely –

The badger who tended him in those long days of recovery seemed sometimes to age and to stand over him, huge and dark, very fierce, just as the Badger himself had been when the Mole first met him. Then he seemed to grow young again, and to help the Mole out of bed that he might be washed, and the mattress turned, and the sheets shaken and then changed, the scent of lavender giving way to the subtle scents of eglantine and balm.

"Ratty –" murmured the Mole, "my friend Ra—"

"Go to sleep, sir. Go back to sleep, for it may be that your friend –"

The gravely ill Mole drifted back to sleep, reaching towards the shred of hope that he found in those few words, "It may be that your friend –"

Another day. The sun slanting across the room, doors opening, voices, and argument.

"I *will* see him, I *must* go to him!"

"It'd be better if you –" growled a deep rough voice.

"But it's Mole, don't you see, my friend M—"

"You're not so well yourself; now come along and go to him later."

"I will see him now. I *must!*"

The door burst open and as the Mole tried to open his eyes against the fierce light of day he heard his name spoken by one whose voice he had thought never to hear again.

"Mole, old fellow, dear Mole, it's –"

"Ratty," whispered the Mole, "you're all right, you're not –"

He felt his hand taken up and held, and he opened his eyes to see his dearest friend staring down at him, shaking his head with wonder and tears in his eyes.

"No, Moly, I'm *not*, and it is only thanks to you and your great courage that it is so."

"But, Ratty, you're all –"

The Rat's face was a good deal thinner than it had been when the Mole last saw him, and it was cut and torn with scratches and bruises, and his left hand was bound in a bandage that would have been a good deal neater and more orderly if the Mole himself had applied it.

"What *happened* to you, Ratty? How did – ?"

Behind the Rat a great shadow loomed, and the Mole saw clearly for the first time the elder of the two badgers who had been looking after him. Then, at the end of the bed the younger, slighter one of the two.

"Mr Brock here says I must not talk to you for too long, Mole, for you have been very ill these weeks past –"

"*Weeks!*" exclaimed the Mole, making a vain attempt to rise from his bed as if to do so might help recover lost time. He collapsed back onto the pillows exhausted.

"Yes, weeks, Mole. You have been seriously ill from the wounds and broken arm and leg you sustained in fighting off that terrible beast from its attack upon me, while I – I –"

Only now did the Mole see how tired the Rat was, and begin to guess how the River must have swept him downstream till exhausted and half-dead he had clambered ashore, lucky to have survived.

"I have been lost in wild woods below this place all this time, too weak even to answer the calls of Mr Brock here, who finally found me only yesterday, never having given up hope I might be alive. But he was only able to bring me back to his home here today. I wanted to see you at once, Mole, I wanted to know –"

It was the Mole's turn now to comfort his friend, and to hold his hand.

187

"Dear Ratty," said he, "we have both come through our ordeal and will get better – but I'm sure that these good gentlemen will be happier if you go and rest now yourself. We shall talk later."

Brock nodded his head approvingly at this, and the younger badger, whom the Mole took to be his son, helped the Rat away.

For a long time then Brock stared down at the Mole without saying anything, and in his younger days the Mole might have been very afraid of his fierce look, of that deep voice, and of his silence. But no more. Rather the contrary indeed, for he rather fancied he knew who the older badger was, and that one important purpose of his journey had in a most unexpected way been fulfilled.

"Your friend," said Brock, "has told me little of who you are, of why you are here, and it may be better for all concerned if you do not speak of it more. You are naturally welcome to stay till you are fully recovered but – well, we do not see many strangers in these parts and prefer it that way. We keep ourselves to ourselves and –"

"Mr Brock," interrupted the Mole, "I believe you may have guessed where we have come from. I believe –"

"And what if I have?" said Brock angrily, pacing about the room as if he were not in the presence of an invalid but an inquisitor, which in a sense he was.

"My name is Mole," he said very simply, "and I live at Mole End along the River Bank."

"Humph!" said Brock.

"And my friend Ratty lives there too –"

"I am not interested in the past or future life of you or your friend," said the badger brusquely, "and I will have discharged my responsibility when I see you both back to health and off on your journey away from here. You should not have come here in the first place. Now, if you have any sense you will go straight back to wherever it is you say you've come from, and you'll avoid using the River till you're a good deal lower down the valley, for the Pike roams all along its length up here."

"And *my* responsibility as leader of this expedition," said the Mole, boldly interrupting again and feeling his spirits rise by the moment, even though tiredness was returning, "is to say what I feel I must to those I feel should hear it. Nobody should be afraid of a few words now and then!"

"Humph!" said Brock once more, glowering furiously and reaching for the door handle.

"Others encouraged us to make this journey, among them Mr Toad of Toad Hall – I believe you may have *heard* of Toad Hall?"

"And what if I have, eh, what then?"

"And also Mr Badger of the Wild Wood – he was very insistent that we embark upon our venture."

If the Mole had any doubts before about the identity of Mr Brock, they were now dispelled, for that large and angry animal stilled at once at the mention of Badger and the Wild Wood, and his hand fell away from the door handle.

"He is still alive?" growled Badger's son.

"He is very much alive," said the Mole, before adding more gently, "and I am permitted to say that he – that he –"

There was much that the Mole might then have said,

but the great animal who stood before him seemed half broken by his words, and by what he might reveal, and he sensed that he must go gently. In any case the Mole felt tiredness sweeping over him and he knew he could not stay awake much longer, or talk very sensibly.

"I want to say only this," he continued. "Earlier this year Mr Badger had reason to look after me in his home much as you have done these weeks past —"

"It has not been your year for good health, Mr Mole," said Brock with the first glimmerings of a gruff and rueful good humour that reminded the Mole of the Badger himself.

"No, it has not," said the Mole. "Badger was kind enough to take care of me, and in the spare room in which he put me he kept certain mementoes of his past — items that I think suggest that but few days can go by when he does not think of the past with some regret, and wish he might redress whatever mistakes he may have made."

"What items?"

"A blue-black overcoat, for example, that might have fitted one not much younger than the badger who has helped me regain my health these weeks past, whom I take to be your son, and therefore Mr Badger's grandson."

"Aah —" sighed Brock, sitting down at last.

"And some worsted trousers, worn once by the same small person, and a hand-knitted red woollen scarf —"

"He still has my red scarf —"

"And a great deal more," said the determined Mole. "For example, he has kept most carefully those books that young person once owned, and which that same person most wilfully scored and crayoned, as young people will —"

"Why," exclaimed Brock, his anger and irritation nearly all gone and the warmth of childhood memory softening his care-worn eyes, "I would very much like to see those books again!"

"And also," continued the Mole, resolutely putting off his tiredness that he might not miss this opportunity of plain talking, but pausing briefly when he saw that the bedroom door had opened a little and Brock's son was outside and no doubt hearing every word, which seemed a very good thing indeed, " – also, Mr Badger has kept upon the wall of that bedroom a calendar which he should long since have removed, whose year I think you might very well recall."

"Of course I *do* remember the year," said Brock quietly, "and the date, too, for it was a Monday, and the last day of September –"

The Mole nodded, remembering how the Badger had written the words "*The Final Date*" upon the calendar against that very day. He was glad to see that when Brock's son found courage to creep into the room, and sit upon the bed in wary expectation that his father would ask him to leave, nothing was said, and he was allowed to stay.

"How I wished that he had come with me," said Brock.

"He followed you some way up-river as far as the Tavern at Lathbury," said the Mole, "but there he learnt of what he presumed must be your death at the jaws of the Pike and –"

Brock nodded wearily and said, "I had an encounter much as you did, and like you was lucky enough to escape with my life. I have stayed up here ever since, with my privacy preserved by the Pike itself. For many years I lived alone till this young – my son's mother graced me with her presence and companionship for a number of years till she – well, of her passing I shall say nothing now."

"Nor have you ever said anything of your other past, father," said the younger badger, "except those tales you told me when I was very young of a place, a beautiful place, called the River Bank, and another nearby, dark and fearsome, to which you gave the name Wild Wood."

"Did I?" said Brock, affecting not to remember.

"He certainly did," said his son, turning to the Mole, "but never more than that, and never once since I grew older and began asking questions."

"Did he not tell you of Badger, a wise animal who lived in the Wild Wood?" said the Mole, sleepy now, and wishing so much that Brock would take up the tale he should have told his son long, long ago.

"Badger? Well, I think perhaps there was such a one in the tales he told –"

"And did he not tell you who Badger was, and is still?" whispered the Mole, looking to Brock with appeal in his eyes, for it was not a story *he* should tell.

"Who *is* Badger then?" said Badger's grandson.

How long and deep the silence then as the Mole slipped back towards sleep, but not so long that he did not hear, or fancy he heard, a voice very like the Badger's own, a little gruff and rough around the edges, but warm at its centre, beginning thus: "It was a long, long time ago when I was very young, and your grandmother was still alive –"

And as the Mole's eyes closed, and he slipped into oblivion for a time, one badger spoke as a younger one listened, and told a tale too long untold, too long suppressed, of the Wild Wood and the River Bank.

Six days later the Rat was very fully recovered, and raring to be up and at it, while the Mole, with some assistance, was able to sit outside Brock's house in the woods near Pike Lake, and stare contentedly at a distant prospect, hazy blue, of mountains and waterfalls none had ever been to, nor would be likely to.

"Aye, Beyond's somewhere up there, all right," Brock told them, "but I've done enough journeying away from things in my lifetime, and I'll leave its exploration for others."

How much they had talked, and how much they had listened, and how much, finally, they had agreed, and resolved.

For it was clear that the Mole would need a month or two yet before his broken bones and wounds recovered sufficiently for him to risk the journey home.

"You can't leave it much beyond autumn," said Brock, "for the winters are wild and rough up here and will do your health no good at all. But you should be well enough to leave by then."

Meanwhile, the Rat was much exercised by the fact that they had been away from the River Bank for a good deal longer than intended, and that by now the Otter and the Badger would be very worried indeed, and quite likely to mount an expedition to rescue them. The more so, because a day or two after he had escaped from the Pike and crawled shivering to some dark hole along the steep-sided River he had thrown some broken beech branches into the water, in the hope that the Otter might eventually see them, and realize that a serious accident had befallen them.

"I had no idea if you were alive or not, Mole, and I felt it the best thing I could do. Well, if Otter sees them he's sure to come upstream, endangering himself and any that come with him. Therefore I must journey back to head him off, and reassure our friends that though an invalid still, you are recovering."

But the Mole would not hear of the Rat setting off alone and the two friends argued the point most fiercely for a time. It was only the wise intercession of Brock himself that produced a compromise – not one that was entirely satisfactory or free of risk, but quite the best that any of them could think of.

"Of course," said Brock, "I have no particular wish to

go back to the River Bank, for those days are over for me. But now I cannot, and will not, deny my son knowledge of his past, and I feel it only right that he should visit the River Bank for a time and meet his grandfather, of whom you have spoken so highly.

"Perhaps in that way old wounds can best be healed. Therefore, I propose the following: I shall accompany Ratty back home now, and see that he arrives safely, without further encounters with pikes or any other beasts. There I shall make my peace with my father. My son here, who is well fitted to look after you, Mole, shall stay here and keep you company.

"I am certain that he will learn much from one as wise and brave as I know you to be, Mole. When you both judge that the time is ripe – but before Autumn I hope – he will act as your guide and guardian, and help you home. It will do him good to have such an adventure, and there comes a time, as I see now nearly too late, that a parent should let his offspring go free."

How gratifying it was to hear Brock talk in this way, Mole told himself, and to see the excitement in his son's eyes at being given a real responsibility.

"But," began the Mole, now sufficiently recovered to allow himself to think beyond the present, and to see certain shadows there, "what of the Lathbury Pike? I mean to say, won't we have to cross the Lake again to get back to the River?"

Brock laughed cheerfully.

"Ratty and I will hike down through the forest and rocks to where you moored your other boat. We will continue from there."

"And what about us?" said the Mole. "I may not be able to hike very far at all."

Grandson laughed.

"Father learnt how to deal with the Pike's teeth many years ago. He built a punt and lined its bottom with copper and hoops of iron."

"The punt we saw by the waterfall," explained the Rat.

"That craft will get us safely downstream when you are well enough to travel," concluded Grandson.

A day or two later the Rat and Brock set off on their long journey and, having said their farewells, Mole and Grandson waved and waved till the travellers could be seen no more.

"Is it a very long way?" said Grandson when they had finally gone.

"It is only as far as you wish to make it seem," said the Mole. "Now let us sit in the sun for a while –"

"And you can tell me a tale of the River Bank."

The Mole laughed and said, "You must have heard them all by now, if not from me then from Ratty, for you have done nothing but make us tell you of our home, so really I –"

"Just one more then?"

The Mole looked at the shadows in the trees, and the distant mountains, and heard the far-off roar of water, and fancied he heard in it a familiar laugh, a loud and braying laugh, a smug self-centred laugh.

"I have told you about Mr Toad, have I not?"

"A few things," said Grandson.

"Did I ever tell you about the time he stole a motor-car and was sent to gaol?"

196

"No!" exclaimed Grandson with delight. "Mr Toad is surely very clever and cunning, is he not?"

"No, he is not," said the Mole severely; "he is very foolish, very vain, very conceited and very mischievous indeed."

"But for all that you like him, Mole, don't you?" said Grandson impulsively.

"For all that," said the Mole, "I *do* like him, and so I will tell you how the infamous business with the motor-car began, and led to Toad's first acquaintance with the Town's gaol."

·X·
In Loco Parentis

Barely had Toad begun his dash for freedom from His Lordship's House, the Madame's son in tow, than he discovered that some unkind person had unleashed His Lordship's hounds after them. He had had dealings with those particular hounds before, and knew them to be slavering and relentless. On the last occasion, since he was not a fox, they had not torn him apart. But this time, as he led the young Count across the lawn, he could not rely on such good fortune.

He had been heading for the creek where he had

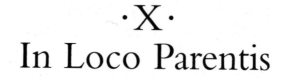

198

hidden his launch, but when he heard that baleful baying and barking he rapidly changed tack and made straight for the River. There, he hoped, the hounds might lose their scent as he and his young friend took to the water and liberty.

It was a close-run thing, and Toad and his ward were but inches from being brought down by the first of the hounds when they reached the River and jumped inelegantly in. The current swept them off downstream and out of harm's way as the confused hounds ran back and forth, wondering what to do.

"Ha, ha!" cried Toad as he floated along. "Have I not fooled them all again? Young sir, you may relax, for you shall be safe with me!"

The Count might very well have wondered about that, seeing as he was now mid-river, cold, and could not swim nearly so well as he could fence but – well – he had to admit that so far it was all much more fun than the chilling formality of the High Judge's House.

"Where are we going, monsieur?" he asked.

"To my motor-launch," gulped Toad happily; "so keep to the right-hand side of the River."

Of their watery arrival at the creek, of their entanglement with what was left of the barbed wire the High Judge had sought to seal its entrance with, and of their eventual clambering aboard the hidden vessel, little need be said. It took longer than Toad expected, and was a good deal colder too, and night had fallen by the time they were dry and safe.

All around them they could hear shouting and see searchlights shining about, and later in the night the ominous sight of a boatload of constables rowing up and down the River beyond the creek's mouth looking for them, and perhaps even dragging the river bottom for their corpses.

"It's a rum go this one," they heard a constable say, "but with a high-class criminal like Mr Toad you can never tell. One thing's sure, it might be better for 'im if 'e is drownded now, for if 'e's not and 'e's caught, 'e'll only be 'anged later."

"Aye, along with that rascal of a French accomplice."

"What are they saying?" whispered the Count whose grasp of constable talk was limited. He was now cold and shivering and not sure any more that this enterprise was quite sensible.

"They are saying," said Toad, who was fortifying himself with a brandy, "that I am a very well-known gentleman and you are a little-known Count."

"What shall we do now, monsieur?"

Thus far Toad's good fortune had not failed him, and for once, perhaps inspired by love for the Count's mother, he showed very considerable resource and common sense.

"No good trying to leave here now, for they'll only hear us. We'll cast off at first light and row silently away up this little stream. It would be unwise to start the engine till we're well out of earshot."

He supped some more brandy and was about to turn in when a strange thought occurred to him, one so unusual that it almost took his breath away. It was brought on by the pathetic sound of the chattering of the Count's teeth. He sat up in surprise and shook his head as if by doing so the thought might be shaken free and take flight elsewhere.

The thought he had concerned the youth and not himself and it was this: that this youngster was shivering with cold and seemed decidedly unhappy and needed – well – needed something more than optimism and the instruction to turn in.

"Here," said Toad, not at all unkindly, "you sound very cold. Can't see you in this dark, but I can hear you and it upsets me."

Then he searched about a bit for a valise of spare clothes Prendergast had put on board in case of emergencies, and found within it one of his old tweed suits.

"Wrap this jacket around you to keep warm. I'll wake you in the morning."

"Thank you, Monsieur Toad," said the shivering youth, struggling into the garment that was several sizes too large, but no less welcome for that, "I am obliged. My mother 'as said you are very famous. For what?"

"O, for a great many things," said Toad grandly, "and I'll tell you all about them in the morning. Now, please go to sleep, that I might do the same."

Toad could not sleep, however, and instead found himself lying awake, listening as the lad's gentle breathing grew deeper, and then deeper and slower still. Then, when the stars came out, and the moon began to rise, Toad found he had no wish to sleep, though the day had been long and onerous, for there was something strangely pleasant in finding himself the watchman over a youth such as he had once been.

Very famous, was he? Well, perhaps he was – no, he *certainly* was – but Toad was suddenly not so sure that dragging this youth into his present misfortunes was admirable at all. It was all very well for *him* to get wet and cold, ride roughshod over others and break the law, but this young toad was –

"Monsieur! I want a drink of water!"

The lad sat up suddenly in the moonlight, the jacket about him, and Toad found himself fumbling around in the cupboards of his craft for a decanter of water he had seen earlier, and which the excellent Prendergast daily renewed.

"Now!" said the spoilt and demanding Count.

"Coming," said Toad, trying to quiet the petulant voice, and rather surprised that when he had filled a glass the youth expected him to feed it to him. When he had finished, and the youth had immediately fallen back to sleep, Toad was very surprised to find himself feeling not irritable and ill-used, but filled with amused affection.

He took up a place near the sleeping youth, and continued to watch the stars and moon, and thought of many things, not least of which was when he was young, long long before, when his father was alive and Toad Hall filled with such life and fun –

"Monsieur, monsieur! I am hungry. Get me my breakfast now!"

Toad was wakened by this peremptory command and discovered that warm and glowing though his feelings towards the youth had been in the night, they were less so, now that morning had come. He had a headache, he saw it was a good deal past dawn, and he heard once more the baying of hounds as they resumed the manhunt.

"No time for breakfast," he cried, "for we must be up and away."

"But always I 'ave breakfast before the servants bathe me," said the youth. "I 'ave it now before we go."

"We go first and have it later," insisted Toad, "otherwise the only place we'll be going to is gaol."

"*Non, non, non!*" said the boy very angrily, thumping the cabin wall with his clenched fist.

"Sssh!" urged Toad.

"I shall go outside and shout for my breakfast if you do not give it to me now!" said his fellow fugitive, whom Toad was rapidly beginning to think might be a very loathsome and spoilt youth after all. But he also saw that he was very determined and would no doubt make a great deal of noise if he did not get his way.

"Well," grumbled Toad, sorting through the galley's cupboards, "I suppose I might make some tea without milk while you eat these dried biscuits, but we must be quick."

"I do not drink your tea, and I do not eat food for dogs."

"Ah!" said Toad, irritated and increasingly alarmed. To the baying of the hounds had been added the shouts of rough-sounding men, more than likely a mixture of constables and gardeners, and Toad wanted to get away more than ever.

"I drink coffee with two croissants, hot but not too hot."

"Coffee?" said the bemused Toad. "Finest Ceylon tea is the best I can do, and perhaps if you put some of this salmon and shrimp paste upon those biscuits –"

"Psah!" said the vile youth.

" – or this delightful English rolled ox tongue, which I will open and spread for you –"

"Food for cats!"

" – or, instead, a teaspoonful from this pot of Colonel Skinner's Chutney (of extra quality and imported) then –"

"'Orrible, monsieur."

" – then," continued the now thoroughly annoyed but increasingly resolute Toad, "your dried biscuits might taste a little nearer to the croissants to which you are accustomed."

"You are a lunatic, monsieur, to suggest such a thing. I know all about English cuisine —"

"In which case," said Toad, whose patience had finally reached its limit, "I suggest you go ashore and demand your breakfast at His Lordship's House!"

That silenced the youth, and gave Toad opportunity to ascend to the deck and deduce that there was no time left for silent rowing. He quickly started the engine and, keeping its roar low, guided his launch out of their hiding place, and gently on up the stream, unseen if not quite unheard.

The youth remained sulking below decks, but Toad's good humour had recovered itself, for the sun was shining, no boats, or hounds, or mounted policemen seemed to be in pursuit, and what lay ahead was freedom and adventure.

Only very much later in the morning did he stop and moor the craft, so that he might go below decks and, ignoring the wretched youth altogether, there make himself some tea, and dig into the excellent hamper of table dainties and other provisions Prendergast had provided. There was even milk of a kind — Diploma Condensed "The best for infants" — and though it tasted strange with the Ceylon tea, back on deck again, with the engine purring beneath him once more and a hot steaming tin mug of the brew in his hand, Toad could not but feel pleased with himself, and with life.

Only in mid-afternoon did the young Count's resolve to sulk finally break, and he asked that he might have a little tea ("since it is tea time") and a few biscuits ("to settle my stomach"). Toad had the sense to provide them without comment. In any case, he felt sorry for the boy, whose eyes were red-rimmed from crying.

For the next three days Toad and the youth battled out their differences: it was impossible for the youth to bathe without hot water and Roger et Gallet soap; it was not proper to utilize the bushes along the bank when nature called; it was absolutely impossible for the youth to take a turn at cleaning the galley and tying up the boat.

"Non! Non! Non!"

But by the third day the youth had become a little hardened to the fugitive's life and Toad felt they were finally making progress: he washed now in the stream itself, he happily followed nature's call in a more rustic way than he had been used to, and he proved a much dabber hand than Toad at keeping the craft ship-shape.

And his eyes were no longer red-rimmed.

"Monsieur Toad, will you tell me of your famous deeds?" he asked on the third evening, and Toad felt a great deal of satisfaction that he did so, for he knew that such differences as there were between them were on the way to being resolved and forgotten.

Toad spoke that evening of motor-cars and flying machines, of injudicious judges and corrupt policemen and ungodly bishops, and a very impressive tale he made of it.

"Now I understand," said the youth, "why you are so famous, for to defeat twelve judges, and to escape one 'undred policeman and to, as you say, unfrock eight bishops is *formidable!*"

"Well, I did not quite mean —"

"Incroyable! I understand why *Maman* —"

"Florentine?" said Toad, thinking of that name for the first time since his flight. "She spoke of me?"

"Like a brother, *Maman* 'as said, or perhaps a father –"

This was not quite what Toad wished to hear, but then – and as night fell, and the youth finally slept, Toad saw that his first flush of love was over and had been replaced by – by – he was not quite sure what.

In the summer days of slow progress that followed – Toad having decided to lie low and keep out of sight and lay the boat up in any enshadowed little creek he could find – the Count began to talk to Toad about himself, his *chère Maman,* his life and – and what a sorry tale he had to tell.

Lonely, spoilt, indulged, too rich too young for his own good, without friends of his own age, and lately dragged from pillar to post by his mother in her pursuit of Art and Creation and with servants at his beck and call wherever he went, he was a decidedly unhappy youth.

Not that the Count expressed himself thus – rather the opposite in fact – and certainly he seemed unaware that it had been boredom, and a toadish instinct for adventure, that had caused him to duel with Mr Toad.

As the days went by Toad recognized more and more something of himself in the young Count, and he had very mixed feelings about it. For it takes a vain, spoilt, unprincipled and conceited toad to recognize another in the making.

Yet, as their chances of discovery receded the further they journeyed upstream, Toad began to see other qualities in the young Count and discovered in himself an unexpected desire to educate the Count in the ways of the world, and considerable pleasure in doing so. Though it must be said that Toad's notion of education was unlike others', and his choice of which qualities to encourage, and which to play down, dangerously personal and eccentric.

For Toad did not quite see things as others did in matters personal, moral and practical.

For example, Toad's approach to the youngster's evident delight in pranks of any kind ("Cut other people's boats' moorings as much as you like, but not mine," said Toad), and behaviour quite unprincipled ("Of course farmers don't mind if you steal a churn or two of milk for it saves 'em the labour of carrying it," claimed Toad), and enjoyment quite unbridled ("Sloe and blackberry? Can't beat Mr Mole's. Claret? Can't beat mine. Last drink were I to be hanged for my crimes? Champagne, courtesy Moet & Chandon, none better!").

Yes, no doubt about it, Toad told himself, the Count has a lot to learn from me, but he is learning it fast, and a few more weeks in my exemplary company and he will be a Toad with a Future!

Meanwhile they were very rapidly running out of supplies, and even Toad was beginning to tire of the fugitive life and to wish for hot baths again and good food, and a bed more comfortable than a ship's bunk.

It was about then that their slow progress finally brought them to that same farmhouse that the Rat and the Mole had visited some weeks before, again at a time when the farmer was away at market.

The hospitable farmer's wife and daughter once more offered the travellers the barn, which had been perfectly adequate for the Rat and the Mole, as it had been for every traveller and itinerant for several hundred years past.

"Ah, madam," said Toad when he was shown these simple quarters, and thinking that here was an opportunity to teach his young ward a thing or two about how to make things work to one's own advantage, "it is kind of you to offer my young relation here such commodious accommodation but alas I cannot accept it on his behalf. No, we shall sit out here on this hard soil, and it matters not that the clucking and crowing of this noisome chicken run will keep us awake, for we shall be content —"

"But, sir," said the farmer's wife, mortified that her hospitality should be made to seem so meagre and unwelcoming, "I assure you —"

"Madam," said Toad, pulling her to one side and winking at the Count, "my young relation here is of a weak and frail disposition, given to fits and other attacks of an unpredictable kind."

"The poor boy!" exclaimed the farmer's daughter in the kind of sympathetic and willing voice that Toad had rather hoped to hear.

"Attacks brought about by the passing of his late father —"

"How tragic!" exclaimed the mother.

"And, in a manner of speaking, the very recent loss of his mother —"

"Woe, woe!" wept the daughter.

"These unfortunate events have meant that he has had to assume the responsibilities of a senior member of the French nobility at far too young an age —"

"You mean he is stable lad to a nobleman or something of the kind, and his master is, or rather was —"

"He may look like a stable lad to you in his present state, but wash and polish him up a bit, dress him in the silks and brocades to which his delicate skin is used, and you will see that you are referring to none other than the Comte d'Albert-Chapelle —"

"He is a Count!?"

"A genuine Count, madam, and you offer him little more than a chicken run for a bed. I know you mean well and perhaps have no better bed in this —"

"Daughter!" cried the good-hearted woman. "These noble gentlemen must have *our* beds while we make do with the settle in the parlour. Let this fair youth have your softer and more comfortable bed, while his elderly relative here can take that of mine and my dear husband's. It is not so comfortable, sir, as you'll be used to, seeing as my husband's Lathbury born and bred and used to rough ways and horsehair mattresses."

"Madam," protested Toad, not much pleased to be called "elderly", but rather more concerned just then that the softer of the beds was to go the Count's way and not his own.

"Of course the young orphan shall have my bed, Mother," said the girl.

"Miss," essayed Toad once more, "I think that in France horsehair mattresses are very much *à la mode* among the nobility and that the Count might prefer —"

But they would not hear of it, and the Count, now to Toad's considerable annoyance acting the feeble part very well and leaning upon the daughter's arm, was led into the house and shown his accommodation for the night, ignoring Toad's mutterings and glowerings.

When morning came the air was filled with the scents of sizzling ham and new-baked bread, and Toad, who had had a comfortable night after all, could not but notice that when the Count finally deigned to make an appearance – it was nearly noon when he did so – he made no mention of coffee and croissants, none at all, but tucked in heartily to all he was offered.

"He seems very well this morning, and to have a hearty appetite," said the farmer's wife, "so perhaps after all you will not wish to stay for a few nights more as we thought you might –"

Toad saw that here was another important lesson for the Count to learn: never look a gift horse in the mouth, or, take all that is offered to you and try to get more if you can.

"It is often when he eats well and looks at his best that he is suddenly taken ill," said Toad mournfully, winking at his young friend that he might understand he had a part to play in this charade. Then, sighing sadly, he continued, "O yes, he usually has one of his turns just when things seem at their best and he at his happiest. A hearty appetite is a bad sign, I fear. Do you feel quite well, Count?"

"I feel very well indeed," said the Count, understanding the game he must play, "and for that reason, Uncle, I am very worried that I may soon be ill."

"O, poor youth, never to be able to enjoy happiness!" said the warm-hearted daughter.

"That is why I am needed," said Toad, "and must be constantly at his side, for I am trained in the doctoring business!"

Toad winked and nudged his ward a few more times, that the Count might have a fit or two, for now was just the right moment, with the ladies wringing their hands, and ready to do anything Toad asked. But evidently Toad had not yet trained his ward in all his cunning, duplicitous ways, for it was only slowly that the penny finally dropped, and he at last realized that he must be ill immediately.

"Mon dieu!" he cried, rather overdoing it, but impressing Toad by his enthusiasm, "I feel do not well!"

"Madam, hot water at once!" cried Toad urgently. "When he mixes up his words like that it is a sign that his mind and vision are becoming confused."

"Not do I well feel at all!" gasped the youth, clutching variously at his throat, his heart, and his stomach since he was not quite sure of the medical meaning of the English words "fit" and "turn".

"Quickly now, miss," commanded Toad, "fetch some towels to wrap about his head and blankets to cover his body which will soon begin to perspire and shake!"

Then – but what more need good honest folk learn of Toad's duplicity, and his speedy corruption of the youngster into his wicked ways. How grievous it is to see Toad thus teaching Madame's child how to play upon the good nature of others for his own advantage. No Fagin ever corrupted youth better than Toad dealt with the Comte d'Albert-Chapelle in the next three days. During which the two toads kept this act up, and had mother and daughter running about at their every whim and command.

The deception might have continued, and the good women been eaten out of house and home, had not the farmer himself come back, understood the situation at once, and turned his unwanted guests out in very short order.

"But, father, he's a real French count," wailed the daughter.

"'E be a real foreign rascal, that's what 'e be!" roared the farmer before turning to Toad.

"Husband, dear, do not treat the old gentleman roughly, for 'e is —"

"O, I know what 'e *is*, right enough, 'e be a scoundrel and the only thing that stops me from giving 'im the proper drubbin' 'e deserves is that at least 'e baint stooped so low as to pretend to be that good and worthy gentleman, that onribble gentleman wot done us all a favour a few years back and fooled that even worse scoundrel the 'igh Judge into giving 'im a bed for the night."

This was rather a long speech, and it was made at some speed and with considerable passion, and Toad was not quite sure he understood the gist of it, except that in some backhanded way it referred to himself.

"You mean — ?" began Toad, sensing some advantage to be taken in all this.

"'E means, sir — and I do beg pardon for my husband and his rough Lathbury ways — that it wouldn't have gone well for you if you 'ad pretended to be Mr Toad of Toad Hall, who is very well regarded in these parts since 'e cocked a snook at our landlord the High Judge and —"

"But I *am* Toad of Toad Hall, and it is from the High Judge that I am once more a fugitive and for which reason I need your help," spluttered Toad, realizing too late that had he said who he was at the beginning he would have got all he wanted and a lot more as well without the need of the deception and posturing of the past few days.

"There you are, wife, what did I say?" roared the enraged farmer. "'E be the vagabond he looks, and is so duplicitous as 'e's claiming now to be Mr Toad hissen!"

The wife screamed and grabbed the nearest broom while the daughter, weeping at the deception she felt she had suffered, took up a copper frying pan, and all three drove the two down to the River and threw them in the water.

"You never come here no more!" cried the farmer.

"Deceiver!" cried the wife.

"Toads!" wept the daughter, and they all went their way.

Once the three had gone, Toad and the Count clambered up the bank once more, boarded their boat again and took it a little way up-river lest they should be assaulted once more.

"All in all," observed the incorrigible Toad later when he had dried out a bit, and made himself a mug of tea, "that was but a small price to pay for four days' free board and lodging. In any case, I was growing weary of the comfort of their home, and their endless female tittle-tattle. It's the freedom of the river once again for us, to go where we will, and live as we must!"

The Count, now thoroughly enjoying his life with

Toad, and forced to agree that the adventures of the past few days were infinitely preferable to the tedium of the stately aristocratic homes to which he was used, laughed merrily.

"But," said Toad a good deal later, "we must realize that this cannot go on much longer. The launch is running out of fuel, and I have very little money. I should not be surprised if that wretched and mean-spirited farmer reports us to the police, not realizing that I am who I say I am – or that it will be the real heroic Toad, on the run merely because of a *crime passionnel*, for which in your excellent and civilized country there is no punishment, whom he will be turning in.

"Either we use our cunning and cleverness to get the launch refuelled and victualled, and proceed further upstream and out of harm's way, or we sell it and purchase some other means of transport!"

"Yes!" said Toad's willing student.

"And sell it for a good deal more than it is worth," added Toad.

"Of course," said the foolish youth, now doomed, it seemed, to follow Toad upon his downward path.

They proceeded slowly, trusting that such fuel as they had would carry them to a place where they might find new fodder to feed the growing appetite of their deceit.

"Ever fished?" said Toad lazily that same evening, when the effects of their last free breakfast were beginning to wear off, and hunger pangs beginning to gnaw. Suddenly dried biscuits seemed unappetizing, and he had memories of fishing with his father in the good old days.

"Never, monsieur," said the Count.

"Nothing to it," said Toad.

And nor, strangely enough, was there.

In addition to the rod Toad had first taken to the boat when he escaped his well-meaning friends at Toad Hall, were the rod and tackle Prendergast had stowed aboard. For bait there were worms in the bank, and lures and flies of all descriptions in the tackle box.

Toad might not be a practical animal in many ways, but just as no boy forgets the lessons received from a piscatorial father by the riverside, of line and trace, of reel and cast, of waiting and of strike, so Toad had not forgotten. Nor had he forgotten the pleasure of watching the River glide by as evening falls, the rise of fish just out of reach, and the first call of tawny owl. Then when the last catch is in, and the rods and tackle stowed, the special joy of the campfire, and the spitted fish which, cooked and garnished with the riverside herbs, surely taste better than any meal ever tasted before.

Such was the Count's introduction to fishing by Toad, and as in all else, the Count proved a willing and able pupil; and by now a grateful one too. Which made Toad happier than he had been for many a long year.

For here were pleasures simple, pleasures lawful, pleasures born not of vanity and conceit and an overweening desire to be clever at the expense of others, but pleasures fairly earned, and fairly enjoyed.

"Monsieur Toad," said the youth later still, his hunger satisfied better than he had ever known before, "today – this afternoon – this evening –"

But one who had been indulged all his life now found he had no easy language with which to express happiness,

nor did he yet know the words "companionship" and "peace".

"Mmm?" said a contented Toad.

They said no more, but rather let the deep slow drift of the River, with the evening light and stars reflected in its surface, do all their talking for them.

A day or two later they passed Lathbury and arrived at the infamous Hat and Boot Tavern. Their brief moment of peace was behind them, for their fuel had all but run out, and they were hungry once more.

"There's always money going begging in a tavern," declared Toad, and without a thought for the consequences led in the impressionable youngster.

A master of such situations, Toad flashed about the last sovereigns he had with him before investing in a round of drinks for the whole house, on the principle that the returns would be plentiful. Nor did he repeat the mistake he had made at the farmhouse earlier on and attempt to hide his identity – the name of Toad of Toad Hall had a good deal of ready credit in these parts.

When he heard, as he very soon did, that the Rat and the Mole had passed that way a few weeks previously he was naturally both astonished and jubilant, for he immediately thought that they would bail him out if need be.

"You look pleased to hear their names, sir, if I may be so bold," said the landlord.

"Pleased? Of course I'm pleased. Mr Rat and Mr Mole are close friends of mine and sterling fellows. Very resourceful those two, and always good to have about the place when there's trouble and difficulty."

"I should think they do know a great deal about trouble and difficulty, seeing as the Pike's 'ad 'em both."

"Aye," added Old Tom, "they be goners, all right, no doubt about it."

"The Pike?" spluttered Toad. "Goners?"

"Swallowed nearly whole, I wouldn't wonder, one after another!"

The landlord and his friends lost no time telling Toad about those items of clothing – hats and boots and so forth – which had drifted down past the Tavern not so long after they had set off.

"Don't say we didn't warn 'em, for we did," said the landlord. "*They*'ll not ever be seen no more."

"My friends dead?" cried Toad, moved to tears and loud lamentations, for he had been very fond of the Rat and the Mole and could not bear the thought of – "You say they've been eaten by a pike?" he whispered.

"The Lathbury Pike, sir. 'Ad 'em for supper and fed anything that was left to 'er brood for breakfast."

"But – but – but I don't believe it!" cried Toad. Nor did he, for the more he thought of the Rat and the Mole, and of their sterling qualities, of their bravery (more than his) and their good sense (more than his as well) and their common decency (O yes, they had much more of that than him) and –

"No! It cannot be!" he declared, drying his tears and finding comfort in conviction.

"I don't suppose," said the landlord, his eyes narrowing as he poured Toad a tankard of the Judge and Jury, "seein' as you're a sporting gentleman, that you'd care to make a wager upon that point?"

"Of course I would!" cried Toad boldly, only thinking a moment later that he had nothing to wager with, and (speaking of common decency as he had been a moment before to himself) it might not be quite nice to wager upon the lives of friends. But then – and now Toad saw advantage in the situation, and a way of getting himself off the hook of extended credit he was caught fast upon at the Hat and Boot (whose best bedroom and parlour he now occupied), or at least of extending said credit a good few days more while he and the young Count made good their escape.

No sooner had this train of thought run through his mind than it had been formulated by him into a clever and ingenious plan which he believed might solve all their problems.

Without more delay, he leapt upon the nearest table and cried, "I know my friends better than any here, and I'll wager my boat against a half guinea from each one of you, that my friends Ratty and Mole are still alive and will return here within twenty-four hours!"

"That's a loser, Mr Toad, sir, for you know as well as we do –"

Toad's wretched plan was this: to wager on the return of his friends, with his launch (very much coveted by the weasels and stoats in the place) set against their money (plus the full refuelling and revictualling of his craft).

Toad hoped that he might string the Tavern's regulars along like this for a few more days and then do a bunk with both the boat, by then serviceable once more, and the stake money, which he had his young assistant collect in a sail bag and keep prominently upon one of the

Tavern tables. It mattered not that the Rat and the Mole were unlikely to make an appearance for Toad's plan to work. Escaping was the thing.

"I'll wager," cried Toad the following evening (when the Rat and the Mole had naturally not appeared), "that they'll be here within forty-eight hours end —"

Which they were not, and Toad found the mood drifting dangerously towards the carnival as it became plain that he would forfeit his boat and be destitute.

The inmates of taverns like the Hat and Boot like nothing better than to see the high and mighty, and the rich and famous, fall on hard times and notorious poverty. Toad was a good fellow, but he was quality after all and not truly one of them, so it was his own hard luck if they had eventually to turf him out upon his ear and take all that he possessed.

"I'll wager —" began Toad two evenings later, but all present knew he must now finally lose. Yet feeling that in addition to the boat he had all but lost to them he had given them a good deal of enjoyment as well, they began to sing "For 'e's a jolly good fellow!" prior to throwing him out and claiming what was theirs, and placed some very heavy, villainous-looking fellows near the door, the windows and by the chimney piece, lest Mr Toad and his assistant with him were foolish enough to try to escape.

Suddenly a very desperate look indeed came into Toad's eyes, and all he could think to do or say was, "Landlord, the next round's on me!" whilst muttering an abject prayer under his breath which went something like this: "Please Ratty and Mole, I am very sorry to have taken your name in vain but I would be much obliged if you would come to my aid now as you have so often in the past."

"You feeling quite all right, Mr Toad?" said the land-lord, winking at his mates.

"Very well," groaned Toad.

"And these friends of yours, they're on their way, are they?"

"Imminently," said Toad.

"Monsieur," whispered the Count, who was beginning to understand the serious nature of their plight, "will your friends *really* come?"

"Of course they will!" cried Toad, taking the tankard from the landlord's grasp and downing its contents with gusto and seeming confidence, "they have never let me down before and will not do so now!"

How the inmates of the Hat and Boot laughed and chortled at such bravado.

"There's none like Mr Toad," they cried. "So let's sing his health once more before we throw 'im in the water, or something worse!"

·XI·
Breach of Promise

The trying circumstances of Toad's flight from Toad Hall in pursuit of the Madame had caused the Badger and the Otter great worry and concern, though no great surprise. Some such foolishness was only to be expected once he had begun to suffer the affliction of Love.

"Mark my words, Otter," the Badger had warned as they watched Toad and his boat disappear upstream, "we shall see that wretched animal in the dock once more, for he will not escape just punishment again. This is an ill day for the River Bank, and marks the moment of a decline in our general standards and reputation which may lead to no good at all. I fear that the road taken today by one such as Toad, given his strong criminal tendency, can lead only to one place: the final punishment of the hangman's noose. And there will be very little we can do about it, very little indeed.

"It may soon be a dreadful fact that all we have left of our friend is an empty and echoing Toad Hall, and a triumphal statue which is no more than a reminder of the empty life of vanity and false pomp that he led."

Badger's fears were amply confirmed all too soon, when they heard the awful news of Toad's antics at His Lordship's House, and his escape with the Count, and the many offences he had thereby committed. In grim confirmation of the seriousness of the matter, a posse of policemen appeared at Toad Hall to lie in wait for Toad's return thinking he might try to steal in one night, for a change of clothes perhaps, or some general help from members of his household.

Grim and gloomy the weeks that followed, with constables hidden in every ditch and behind every tree, each one suspicious of the River Bank residents, and the likelihood that they would help Toad if they could.

This was made all the worse by the continuing absence of the Rat and the Mole, and the Badger retreated to his home with instructions to the Otter that he should be disturbed only when more news was received. While Prendergast, now much concerned himself, could only proceed with that matter he had promised Toad he would accomplish, which was making preparations for the Grand Opening of the new Toad Hall, set now for the last day of September.

But how hollow and sad it felt to be ordering balloons and bunting, to be arranging marquees and catering, and to be planning fêtes, jousts, and jamborees upon the estate of a master whose feet might, by the time the Opening's due date arrived, already be dangling three feet above the ground, and so find it a little difficult to fulfil his proper function of cutting the ribbon and beginning the celebrations.

Yet none of this appeared in Prendergast's eyes. While the Badger stayed silent in his home, the Otter daily watched the River and roads for news, and all those other creatures along the River Bank waited with bated breath for news of Toad, and Rat and the Mole, Prendergast, the butler *par excellence*, continued with his duties, seemingly unperturbed.

"It certainly looks ill for Mr Toad," he conceded on those nights that the Otter called in and shared a glass of sherry in the butler's pantry, "but I believe that in the end he *will* triumph over his present troubles. I really do." Which words the Otter tried to find comforting.

This oppressive sense of waiting for further news that must inevitably be bad continued through August, and finally into September, with even Prendergast beginning to accept that his arrangements for the Grand Opening on the last day of the month might need to be postponed, or cancelled altogether.

But it was news of the Rat and the Mole that came first, and it was grim. One of the Otter's rabbit spies came rushing to his residence with the news that broken beech twigs had come down-river in sufficient quantity and manner to leave in no doubt that this was one of the pre-arranged signals from the Rat, and one that told of danger and disarray.

"It certainly looks bad," said the Otter, who went immediately to see the Badger, "but we must not act hastily. I talked with Ratty of this eventuality and we agreed that the last thing anyone wants is a rescue party rushing all over the place causing panic, confusion and endangering itself. This signal tells us that they have run into difficulties, and to watch and wait for further news."

"We shall wait a fortnight then," agreed the Badger.

While the Badger and the Otter fretted for their friends, Madame d'Albert had not been idle. The truth was – or had been – that she would have been no more than flattered and amused by Toad's protestations of love, first at Toad Hall and later at His Lordship's House, if that had been the extent of his transactions there.

She enjoyed Toad's amatory antics in the same spirit as any widowed lady likes such attention, regarding swooning swains, floral gifts, and preposterous proposals of marriage from mature gentlemen who should know better as no more than her due, and a pleasant diversion from the daily toil and moil of life.

But in the fatal moment that Toad had leapt to the defence of her son (than whom in Madame's eyes there was no better child in the whole world, nor one more deserving of being granted every material indulgence he asked for, always provided he did not make too many demands of a more genuinely maternal kind upon one whose Artistic Muse was now her only *raison d'être*) her regard for Toad had taken a more serious turn.

Not that Madame had previously desired to be wed again, for the daily practical inconvenience of a son was quite enough without adding to it the responsibilities of caring for a husband.

But the Madame was sufficiently aware of her maternal shortcomings to appreciate how helpful it might be to have at her side a male companion to take from her the responsibilities of entertaining a growing lad, one who through the recent peripatetic years of travel in the cause of Art had become wilful, spoilt, over-indulged and generally troublesome, as youths very often do, rich or poor.

In addition to this practical aspect, Toad's selfless actions on behalf of her son had touched something deep within her heart. Here, it seemed, was a gentleman who did not regard her son as an obstacle to be overcome and pushed to one side on the way to the fulfilment of his passion for herself; here was a swain who might have escaped to safety if he had wished, but who instead risked his life and liberty for the one upon whom she doted more than any other.

Here was one worthy of such love as she had to give, and now suddenly found she *wished* to give. Here, in short, was one whom Madame now wished impulsively and passionately to make her own, and intended to make her own, and certainly would make her own. Someone whose physical form she might also, while she was at it, turn into the greatest sculpture expressive of imperial triumph she had ever made. Thus, all unwittingly, Toad's impulsive action at His Lordship's House had done more than a thousand declarations of love might do, and ten thousand stolen bouquets.

Had Toad known this, and even half suspected the energy and resolute determination that the Madame put into any projects she took under her wing, including love, he might very well have started having nightmares featuring predatory female spiders in webs, or Amazons battling for their puny mates, or even dragonesses luring kindly gentleman-dragons into escape-proof lairs, which might have made unpleasant dreams of incarceration in the Castle dungeon seem positively benign. But Toad did not yet know of the change in her heart, and for the time being at least could continue to sleep relatively easily at night.

Meanwhile, unable to devote herself directly to the fugitive Mr Toad of Toad Hall, the Madame was putting all her impressive energy into negotiating a lifting of all charges against him and her son. She had taken very ill, very ill indeed, the appalling assault by various constables, clerks and clerics upon her little boy, and the moment Toad had escaped with him, she had protested loud and long to the High Judge, the Commissioner of Police and the Senior Bishop over the matter, and even more concerning the subsequent hue and cry which had turned into a manhunt complete with a pack of vicious hounds and rough brutish men with shotguns normally used for shooting plump pheasants and despatching foxes.

At first things had not gone well, and she found herself ignored. Even the threat, which she had regarded as ultimate, that if they did not call off their hunt for Mr Toad and the Count forthwith she would never in any circumstances complete the statue the three had commissioned from her, fell on deaf ears, though the gentlemen did express some disappointment and asked her to reconsider.

"Madame," the High Judge had said chillingly, "I shall regret it if you do not proceed with the work, but we cannot very well set ourselves up as the models, the literal models, for Justice, Law and the Established Church and at the same time allow such a pair of criminals as this Mr Toad of Toad Hall and your delinquent son to roam free of retribution and terrorize the land!"

"But he is only a boy and he is my son," wept the Madame, feeling that a show of tears might help.

"He is a juvenile criminal and you should be at least reassured to know our criminal code is gentler than your own country's for one such as him. There I believe he would be confined in solitary confinement upon Devil's Island for a minimum of sixty years, while here we are more relaxed and I estimate that he will get no more than thirty years or so in Dartmoor Prison for the crimes he has committed, with maternal visits allowed once every two years."

"But, monsieur," she continued, trying a different tack, "these crimes as you describe them were committed only in the course of a passionate moment made wild by the extreme emotions my cousin feels for me. Does not a *crime passionnel* have a special place in your law? Mr Toad and my son, they did it for love! Is that not mitigating?"

"Love mitigating?" responded the High Judge with a bleak laugh. "Why, in our courts the plea of love mitigating and extenuating is very rarely to be recommended, as it is generally taken as a sign of the feeble mind so characteristic of the more violent criminal classes, so I strongly advise you not to use it for the defence. Mere mention of that passion you call love as having been involved will at least double the length of these criminals' sentences and in the case of capital punishment (which I must warn you is a very likely sentence in the case of the infamous Mr Toad) it will be taken as evidence sufficient to speed up to a matter of a few hours the execution once such sentence is passed."

"Monsieur!" said the Madame, now distressed and outraged. "Is there nothing I can do?"

"Appeal to your nation for help, to your Government, to your country's President himself and perhaps, madame, if he comes cap in hand to our monarch then sentences might be reduced by a month or two and your visiting rights improved to as much as once a year."

The High Judge, like so many such eminent personages of the male gender who are of advanced years, was a poor judge of female passions, and a worse politician. The Madame was so incensed by what she heard that she straightway went to the Town and called upon the French Ambassador, waking him from his slumbers with her tale of national insult and aggression against the French nation in the form of one of its most ancient families, namely the d'Albert-Chapelles, and the person of one of that family's most sweet and innocent members.

Here was a clear case of the Anglo-Saxon hordes crossing the Channel once more and inflicting cruel and grievous harm upon the women and children of Gaul. The Madame spoke most eloquently, for even as the initial search for Toad and his accomplice upon his escape was adjourned, the diplomatic wheels of state were set in

motion, and by dawn a telegraphic message lay upon the bureau of an official, a very senior official of the Elysée Palace, the residence of the President of France and all its colonies.

Such matters generally take two or three years to set in motion, but so serious was this one taken to be that within a matter of weeks, which is to say about the time that Toad had reached the Hat and Boot Tavern and had begun his absurd wagers concerning the Mole and the Rat's return, the President of France had taken action and instructed a personal emissary to call officially upon the Court of St James and let his feelings be unequivocally known.

Within hours of that Court's haughty response, which foolishly made mention of Agincourt and Waterloo, and the unimpressive performance of the Gauls against the Romans, French warships were afloat in the Channel, and soon after that the guns of various frigates and destroyers were trained upon those symbols of national pride, the white cliffs of Dover and its Castle.

Over the exchanges that then ensued between ambassadors, generals, synods, national newspapers, hastily convened war cabinets and finally, and most decisively, between the Monarch and the President themselves (just then about to meet mid-Channel to put their respective seals upon an agreement concerning mutual economic and cultural endeavour, a proceeding now seriously jeopardized) a veil of secrecy must be cast for one hundred and fifty years, as is the custom in matters such as this.

But a solution was found, an accommodation made, a compromise agreed, so that Mr Toad of Toad Hall and his accomplice were exonerated, and an exchange of medals between the Royal Society and the Légion d'Honneur to a variety of judges, commissioners of police and bishops made.

In brief, the unfortunate incident regarding Mr Toad, and the insult to France in the person of the Comte d'Albert-Chapelle and the Dowager Countess, the Madame, was hushed up in the interests of everybody and every state concerned.

Thus it was that at the very moment that Mr Toad stood up in that infamous Tavern near Lathbury to make his final wager, he and his assistant were being pronounced innocent and cleared of all charges that arose from the incident at His Lordship's House and, with the final proviso that Madame now agreed to proceed with that work of art she had begun that was to represent and laud the power of the Law, the majesty of Justice and the uplifting spirit of the Established Church, the matter was satisfactorily settled all round.

Not, of course, that Toad could be immediately informed since no one knew where he was, but the constabulary were already on the alert for him and, when he was finally tracked down he could be told the good news and permitted to return home in safety, and as something of a hero.

It was Prendergast who first heard the news that all charges against Toad were to be dropped, and he hurried over to the Badger's house to share it.

"As a matter of fact, sir, the news is both good and bad, if I may so put it. I received a telegraphic message this morning from Madame d'Albert-Chapelle the gist of which is that Mr Toad has indeed been exonerated at the highest levels and no charges are to be placed against him."

"That's a relief," declared the Otter.

"He'll be more conceited than ever after this," growled the Badger. "And the bad news?"

"I think that the Madame's message, with which I fear she had no help in its drafting from a fluent English speaker, makes things all too plain, sir," said Prendergast, handing the message to the Badger.

He read it in silence first, his frown deepening as he did so, and then he read it aloud in its entirety.

> *"My cousin the eroic Monsieur Toad is chased no more and free. The governments of la France and Grande Bretagne have declared him liberated of crimes against His High Lordship.*
>
> *"I, Madame d'Albert-Chapelle, have accepted his proposition of marriage. I arrive today to make arrangements for our grand wedding for 30 septembre. Be ready and be happy for your master and your new mistress."*

The expression on Prendergast's face betrayed nothing of the gloom he must have felt.

"Naturally, sir, I cannot act in any matter except at my master's direct instructions, but since the good lady has been a guest before I can hardly refuse her visit now. Naturally, too, if it is indeed so that she and Mr Toad are officially affianced then – well – arrangements for nuptials can be addended to the plans for the Grand Opening at the end of the month with no real difficulty."

"Is there nothing we can do?" said the Otter. "If only

Ratty and Mole were here they could help us knock some sense into Toad's silly head when he returns."

The Badger sighed and then managed a smile.

"I dare venture that if the Madame is determined for these nuptials to take place then there is little we can do but put a brave face on it and attend the wedding and be as happy as we can for our friend. It is Prendergast here who has his work cut out. I cannot think he relishes the Madame as, as she puts it, his future mistress."

Prendergast rose up and made for the door.

"It really is no trouble, sir, to help one such as Mr Toad for whom I have a high regard."

"You have, haven't you, Prendergast?"

The butler allowed himself a brief smile, just as the Badger had.

"I think I betray no confidence, sir, nor cross any boundaries of propriety when I say that in all my long years of service in many great houses I have never found a post as demanding, as challenging, and as satisfactory in every regard, as that I now enjoy with Mr Toad. He does me great honour employing me, sir; I should lay down my life for him were it necessary."

The Badger and the Otter were both much impressed by this speech, but the Otter could not help adding, "I would be careful about talking about laying down your life, Prendergast, for Toad is capable of almost anything and might drive you to it yet."

"Well, sir, the butler's code is very clear on that partic-ular point for its fifth Article makes so bold as to suggest that, 'if the Master's life is threatened it shall be the duty of a professional butler to offer his life first, which, if accepted, shall be repaid with an honorarium of one week's holiday prior to said life's cessation, if that is practical, but if not a pension of ten pounds a year for life for a named surviving relative or, failing that, a capital sum of one hundred pounds to be donated to the Retired Butlers Benevolent Fund'."

"Most generous," said the Otter with some irony.

"I am pleased you think so, sir," said Prendergast with some satisfaction, "since I drafted that particular Article in the Code myself."

The Madame appeared that same day and, as the Badger predicted, very rapidly arranged matters much as she wished. She and Prendergast maintained a working relationship at least – she effusive with her thanks and ruthless in her purpose of seeing the marriage arrangements made, he economical and noncommittal in his transactions with her, and keeping his master's options as open as he could.

It did not help that Toad had put his proposal of marriage in writing, for there is something incontrovertible about the written word, especially when it reads, *"Sweet Coz, marry me how when and where you like, for I love you till the end of the earth and the moon and –"*

Prendergast did not need to read the rest: the terms of his master's proposal were self-evident, and there was precious little that he could do about it, even had he wished to.

But then, perhaps he did not, for the sincerity of the Madame's affection seemed apparent, and so bountiful were her energies that once arrangements had been made she diverted herself by commencing work upon the statue of her lord and master to be, executing it in the privacy of a spare morning room in the north wing of the Hall.

"And what are these marriage arrangements exactly?" asked the Otter on one of his evening sojourns in the butler's pantry.

"It would seem, sir, that the Madame has friends in high places. The Senior Bishop himself is to conduct the ceremony as part of the proceedings of the Grand Opening; indeed, they are its highlight. The Bishop has granted a special licence, and a dispensation too, so that the ceremony can take place upon the Hall's terrace, which shall for the occasion be deemed to be hallowed ground. The High Judge shall give the Madame away, and the Commissioner of Police is to be chief usher."

"Are you sure that Toad, even if he comes back in time, will be pleased with such arrangements?"

"I hazard that my master will regard them with considerable amusement and enter into the spirit of things."

"Humph!" said the Otter. "Things will never be the same if this goes ahead. What about your own position once the Madame is installed at the Hall?"

"Well, sir," said Prendergast equably, "I think perhaps you are not aware that I took my position here for only six months, which period ends on the last day of October, by when Mr Toad and his spouse will be back from their honeymoon. I shall then depart to an honourable retirement in Australia where I have it in mind to start a small enterprise."

"You are a remarkable man, Prendergast," said the Otter

with admiration. "What enterprise had you in mind?"

"Exports and imports, sir," said Prendergast cryptically.

"Then all we can do is to sit and wait, and hope that Toad hears that he is no longer wanted by the law and returns home in time for his own wedding."

"Indeed, sir."

All of these events, for good and ill, were naturally quite unknown to the Rat as he proceeded on his journey home with Mr Brock, having left the Mole by Pike Lake in the care of Grandson.

A week or so after leaving, and having recovered the small boat from its hiding place, the Rat and Brock finally came within sight of the Hat and Boot Tavern at Lathbury. Their journey had been slow, and not entirely comfortable, for Brock was a good deal bigger than the Mole, and made an ungainly passenger.

"What we need is a bigger boat," the Rat had said more than once with considerable feeling, "and in Lathbury we shall endeavour to find one."

Their surprise can therefore be well imagined when, arriving at the jetty by the Tavern where they intended to moor their battered craft, they found its entire length, and all its mooring points, taken up by a craft many times the size of theirs, and a good deal more ostentatious and imposing.

While through the open door and windows of the Tavern came the sound of raucous inebriated merriment, which resolved itself into cheers, and laughter, and finally a loud rendition of "For he's a jolly good fellow!"

"Obviously we have arrived on a festival day of some

kind," said the Rat, "and perhaps one of the participants is having a birthday and has bought a round of drinks. Let us go and see."

As they approached the Tavern, they saw that a large group of weasels and stoats, all with brimming tankards in their hands, were clustered at the door and windows, for the place was obviously too full to accommodate them.

They therefore could not immediately see for whom the song was being sung. Only as the last notes died away did the Rat hear a braying laugh, which had a very familiar ring to it, and the cry, in a voice even more familiar, "More! Drinks for everybody are on me!"

"But it cannot be!" exclaimed the Rat, eyeing that flamboyant motor-launch.

"What cannot be?" asked Brock.

"That triumphant laugh! That spoilt and conceited voice! If I am not much mistaken that is Toad of Toad Hall himself. And, if I am not still more mistaken he is up to a prank or trick of some kind which will reflect ill upon any who identify themselves as coming from the River Bank. Therefore —"

The Water Rat and Brock slid anonymously inside the Tavern and kept in the shadows to see if he was right.

There was Toad standing upon a wooden table, tankard in one hand and a cigar in the other, leading the rabble in their fun and games. As the Rat arrived unseen Toad held up a hand to silence them, and all was still.

"Come on, gentlemen," he was saying, "place your bets one last time!"

"But, Mr Toad, sir, you've made the same wager each time and each time you've lost! Those friends Mr Mole

and Mr Rat are long since dead and won't never come back. Why, we've won that launch o' yours three times over at least –"

"And I say – double or quits! Or are the good men of Lathbury ungentlemanly cowards and knaves who cannot hold their liquor or honour their debts?"

The Water Rat, the most practical of animals, saw at once that Toad had been so insufferable as to lay wager upon the life of himself and the Mole, but then at least it showed a certain confidence he liked. The Rat was not without a sense of humour, and he saw that his help was needed. Instructing Brock to delay a minute or two and then announce that Mr Toad's friends had just that moment arrived outside, he slipped back to the jetty, tied his own boat to what must surely be Toad's launch and then set the engine running for a speedy departure.

Brock had the same commanding presence as the Badger himself, and when he emerged from the shadows and made the announcement a general exodus ensued. Out came Brock and Toad, with the young Count carrying the money, pursued by a wondering rabble who were astonished at the news that the Water Rat was there.

"Quick!" said Brock to the youngster, and together they heaved Toad aboard, leapt on after him and the Rat expertly powered the craft into the middle of the stream and out of the mob's reach.

"'E's got our money!" cried the landlord.

"'E's got our *beer* money," cried another.

"Aye, so 'e 'as," said Old Tom, his voice strong against

the rabble's, "but didn't 'e win 'is wager fair and square? That's certainly the same rat as we saw before, if I'm not mistaken."

"You're a rascal, Mr Toad! I'll bet you knew Mr Rat was alive all along!"

Toad, now nearly recovered and realizing he was safe once more, assumed a mysterious smile, a most satisfied smile.

"Did I win it or not?" he cried, grabbing the money from Brock and holding it aloft.

"You did, sir," they cried in reply. "But now you've got the boat as well. It don't seem quite fair."

Toad laughed.

"Am I not the cunningest, the cleverest, the wiliest Toad who ever lived?"

The mob stared at him, lost for words.

Finally it was Old Tom who spoke for them all.

"I'll tell you what you be, sir," said he, with admiration in his voice. "You're a toss-potly stuff-gutly vagabond, the finest as ever darkened the doors of the Hat and Boot, and you be welcome hereabouts anytime!"

There was general laughter at this and Toad replied, "Well spoken, my man! Here, landlord, take this back and let everybody have another drink on me!"

With that the generous and good-natured Toad swung the bag of money about his head and hurled it back onto the bank where it fell at the landlord's feet.

Then, turning to the Rat, he calmly said, "You arrived barely in the nick of time, old chap; what kept you?"

"But —" began the Rat furiously.

Quite unashamed and betraying not a single trace of

gratitude, Toad commanded the Rat thus: "Steersman, guide her from these shores!"

At this there was a general hurrah for Toad and all his works, except from the Rat, who looked as if he would have a good deal to say on this subject and some others concerning Toad before very long.

As they set off downstream it was to another rendition of the familiar song, only this time it began, "For *Toad's* a jolly good fellow!" and it continued long and loud and saw the launch and its passengers well on their way.

But that evening, when the boat and its occupants were out of harm's way and had been properly introduced to each other, the Rat interrogated Toad long and hard. He heard the sorry tale from its lunatic beginning to its wretched end, and he saw how dreadful and baleful an influence Toad had been upon his youthful ward.

"Toad," said the Rat finally, after due consultation with Mr Brock, of whom Toad had been very much in awe from the moment he heard he was Badger's son, "I will not allow this to go on. You cannot continue to be a fugitive and corrupt this young person. You must try to set an example."

"I will, of course I will," said Toad. "Just let us off the boat – for I do not like the direction in which you are going – and I will promise always to be good, and never to lead my friend astray. We will –"

"It is not good enough, Toad, and if Badger were here, and Mole as well, I know what they would say."

"They would be more understanding than you, Ratty," said Toad.

"They would be *as* understanding as me, not more so," averred the Rat. "I want you to set the only example you can to this poor, corrupted youth and come along with me and give yourself up."

"But they will punish me, Ratty," said the terrified Toad. "I know they will –"

"So they may, and a good thing too. You must take your chances, for it is the only proper course to take."

How desperately Toad looked about the decks for a means to escape, how pathetically he wept and pleaded to be allowed to flee, if only by himself.

How predictable the final dash he made for it, attempting to leap from the bows to the nearest bank and falling into the water.

They fished him out with a boathook and dried him off, and, then, not trusting him further, he was tied up struggling in the fo'c'sle, little better than a mutineer, with the large solid form of Mr Brock watching over him.

Then, unwilling to delay more, the Rat took up the wheel and set course for home.

Toad's terror at the prospect that awaited him once he gave himself up very rapidly increased the nearer to the River Bank they got, as did his pleadings and offers of money to the Rat to let him go. But the Rat would not, though he released him from his bonds when he seemed to have calmed down.

When the Rat finally guided the craft round the last corner of the River before Toad's estate, there, as Toad cowered behind the gunwales, covering his face against his enemies, seeking to cover his eyes and ears against their imminent commands for him to put his hands behind his back so that handcuffs could be put upon them, a very remarkable sight unfolded.

News of their arrival seemed to have gone ahead of them so that several boats were in the water, filled with cheering people, and bunting had been hung among the willows along the banks. While upon Toad's boat-house hung a huge bill board upon which were written these remarkable words, "WELCOME HOME, MR TOAD! HERO AND HUSBAND TO BE!"

Toad heard the commotion of his welcome, mistook it for the sound of arresting officers, and dived below decks in an attempt to win a few more seconds of liberty. While up above the Rat was very quick to size up the situation, and expressed himself not at all pleased with it. Worse, he saw that the young Count's admiration for Toad was growing once more.

He went below to break the news to Toad.

"I am not to be arrested after all?" cried Toad. "Not thrown into gaol?"

"No, Toad, you are safe, it seems."

Toad stood up and peered through a porthole, and saw the cheering crowds of the estate's staff, at whose head stood Prendergast.

"O, and am I not *clever*?" brayed Toad. "Am I not brilliant in all I do?"

Though happy for Toad in one way, the Rat could only glower at this rather unseemly display of smug self-satisfation, and the deleterious effect it must be having on the young Count. Brock, on the other hand, looked very bemused, for this was not the homecoming to the River Bank that he had expected, and Toad Hall looked very different from what he remembered.

But thus did Toad return home and seemed to confirm yet again that Fate was eternally with him, and against all that is just, and proper, decent and good.

Yet, just as he was about to put his foot upon his property once more, his hand steadied by the inestimable Prendergast, he paused and said, "What's that?"

"Sir?"

"That notice. It says rather more than 'welcome home' and 'hero', does it not?"

"It does seem to," agreed Prendergast.

"It also says 'husband to be'," said Toad darkly. What distant shadow shifted then within his heart, and what caused him to look beyond the bank and up towards the house and its attendant terrace? Upon which he saw a strange effusion of flowers and silk which, unaccountably, reminded him of an exotic waiting spider in her web.

"Am I to be married?" said Toad in some surprise.

"See, your lady awaits you," said Prendergast, pointing to the terrace.

Flowers, that was what Toad could now make out, roses mainly. In the shape, the ghastly shape, of a red heart in whose midst a female form seemed to move and wave.

"What is that?" said Toad, frozen to the spot.

"The Madame has seen fit to prepare a romantic tableau for your return," said Prendergast, "with herself at its very heart."

"O, well, I suppose we must humour her for now," said the ungrateful, fickle Toad. "But then, Prendergast, an engagement is one thing, marriage another. Why, we need not do the deed for months yet, even years –"

With that Prendergast pushed his suddenly unwilling master up the steps to the terrace where, despite all Toad could do, he was swept up into the Madame's plump arms, and assaulted by the scent of powder and of perfume, of roses and of orchids, and a multitude of kisses.

As he struggled to break free and gasped for air he felt as one who had journeyed far to regain his liberty, only to have it cruelly snatched away once more.

Yet if the astonishing news of Toad's last-minute pardon and return to Toad Hall gave everybody along the River Bank reason to celebrate, the final return of the Mole and Badger's Grandson was the icing on the cake.

It was Otter who brought the news that his spies had seen the Mole and Grandson. They arrived that same evening, drifting gently down in Brock's punt, expertly guided by Grandson. Everyone saw how thin the Mole had become, and that when he stepped from the boat onto the bank, he limped a little, and needed the help that the Rat quickly gave.

"Well," he said, looking at them all with joy, "I am home again at last, home where I belong."

"And this – ?" began the Badger gruffly, looking at the young badger who handled the punt so well.

"Yes," said the Mole, "this is your grandson, Badger, and a very good one he is, as you'll very soon discover."

Badger found that he was looking into the eyes of one very near his own size, who had about him all the youthful grace and good humour of her whom the Badger had once loved dearly, and which any grandparent would have been glad to see so evident in a younger generation.

Perhaps nothing in all of the Badger's life had moved him so deeply as that meeting, and if Grandson looked shy and uncertain, so too did he.

"Why," said the Badger, looking from Grandson to his own son Brock and then back again, with tears filling his eyes, "he – you – you remind me of someone your father and I once loved very much indeed, very much. I – yes –"

If the hug the Badger impulsively gave his grandson then was a little clumsy, and felt a little strange, it was none the worse for that, and nobody chose to notice as he turned away for a moment to wipe some of those tears away and collect himself.

"He's a fine boy, eh, Mole?" he said a little hoarsely once he was himself again, and he said it with a good deal of pride; and perhaps with saying it, the rift between himself and his own son was healed.

"He certainly is, Badger," replied the Mole with a good deal of feeling, for he had come to know Grandson well, and to like him greatly.

"Well then," said the Badger, not at all sure what to do or say next, "well –"

"I dare say, Badger," suggested the Mole judiciously, "that you will wish to show your grandson something of your home in the Wild Wood, for I believe he is very much looking forward to seeing it; and he wants to tell you about our journey here."

"Yes," said the Badger, "that is a very good idea, and I was just about to suggest it myself –"

It was not often that the Badger was lost for words, but upon that happy occasion he was, and as he led his kith and kin off to his home, he felt grateful for the Mole's easing of the situation.

For the next few days, the Badger, Brock and Grandson kept very much to themselves in the Wild Wood. While the Rat saw the Mole safely back to Mole End with the Otter, and there shared a succession of feasts that Nephew had prepared which were in all the warm traditions of the kind of welcome, and the food and drink, for which the Mole himself was renowned.

* * *

Toad found that the six days before his nuptials swept very quickly past, like dried leaves upon an autumn wind. Then he was awakened one morning by Prendergast and all in a horrible daze found himself thrust into a morning suit, handed silk gloves and a top hat and then dragged out onto the terrace of his house, by the Badger, who was, it seemed, his best man.

"But —" whispered Toad, breaking out into a sweat at the very unwelcome sight of wedding guests at his own marriage.

"If there was a way out, old fellow, I would not be against it," said the Badger; "but there is none now and you must accept your fate."

"But —"

"If only you had not put your proposal in writing then perhaps we could have found a way —"

"But, *please*, Badger!"

"Then again, even that obstacle might have been over-come had not the Madame pre-empted all escape from this arrangement by persuading the High Judge himself to give her away, and having none other than the Senior Bishop officiate at the service, while the Commissioner of Police is Senior Usher and —"

"This way, gentlemen," said the Senior Usher at that moment, "those four constables will show you where to stand —"

As Toad followed them he felt even more than before that this was no wedding, it was an arrest and he was now on the way to the final sentencing.

"B-b-but I don't love her, Badger, and I don't think I ever did. It was the idea of Love that I liked, the dreams and poetry, the partings and the returnings, the mooning and the rushing about, but not *this* –"

"Really, Toad," said the Badger with some asperity, "and you might do a great deal worse. Why, I have become quite fond of the Madame myself, everyone has. In any case, there is nothing we can do – why, even Prendergast could think of no solution, for if you do not go through with it then it is quite certain that the Madame will file a suit against you for Breach of Promise and, well, with such important people upon her side, so to speak, and all your previous pardons set aside, then I fear – I greatly fear –"

Just then there was a blast of trumpets and clapping and cheering from the special guests upon the terrace, which was then taken up by the many others in the garden below who had come to enjoy the Grand Opening and, in particular, Toad's wedding, which was generally regarded as the momentous highlight of the day's events, in fact the event of the year!

"She's coming! Look, she's coming on the arm of the High Judge himself —"

"Badger!" pleaded Toad one last time.

Which appeal failing (for the Badger grasped his arm yet tighter), Toad turned to his friends nearby: "Ratty and Mole, can you not help me?"

But they could only shake their heads and urge Toad to put a brave face on it as the Senior Bishop took his place, bible in hand and bishops all about him, and the Commissioner of Police stood near him to one side. Finally the bride to be, dressed in pinks and whites and apricots, approached from within the Hall, upon the arm of the High Judge himself.

"Is there no one who can help me now?" whispered Toad, his eyes wild, and his limbs all shaking. "No one to pity me?"

Yet, as he lowered his head in despair, there *was* one there who seemed fully to comprehend the terror that poor Toad felt, for he too had been oppressed by the many not long since, and he too had come to understand the true value of the liberty that Toad was about to lose. He, too, knew better than any there the difficulties and awfulness of actually living with Madame.

This solitary saviour was Madame's son, the Count.

Callow and young, foolish but brave, he saw Toad's plight and did what he felt he must do. Wresting a crook from the nearest bishop, he leapt in front of Toad and uttered the cry that Toad had made on his behalf in *his* moment of doubt and weakness: "*Liberté, monsieur! Fraternité et Liberté!* Flee, Monsieur Toad, while I fight these cruel men off! Run while you can!"

Toad heard this valiant call to action, and he saw the brave youth who uttered it; and he needed no second thought, nor further encouragement. As his fiancée came out onto the terrace, when all attention was upon her and the High Judge, Toad turned and fled as fast as his short legs would carry him.

As he went he hurled off anything that might be an encumbrance to flight: the carnation in his lapel, his morning coat, then his top hat, and finally his cravat, that he might puff and pant more freely as he fled.

Round the side of the Hall he went, past the vast assemblage of motor-cars and broughams gathered there, and straight out of his own front gates, which he reached just as the first hue and cry was heard.

Above him he saw the notice that the Badger had caused to be set up, and knew beyond doubt the truth of what it said, and that his liberty could not last long.

"THERE WILL BE NO SECOND CHANCE!"

Nor could there be, he knew that now, but while he had life he might have hope, and while he felt hope he could strive to recapture liberty!

Thus Toad fled his own wedding, and left the Madame standing, if not at the altar then upon the terrace, which is the next worst thing; and if any there had ever doubted

254

the truth of the expression "Hell hath no fury like a woman scorned" they needed only to look upon the jilted Madame's face.

"Monsieur?" she wondered.

"Monsieur?!" she wept.

"*Monsieur!*" she bellowed, giving chase at once.

Over the Iron Bridge Toad fled and thence into the Wild Wood. No plan had he, no clever means of escape, just the overwhelming desire to escape the eternal bond that marriage to the Madame, worthy though she was, seemed to be.

While behind him, gathering momentum under the Madame's lead, Toad Hall was in uproar, with constables who had been ushers taking up their batons again. Those among them trained in the handling of hounds and bull-dogs, using Toad's cravat for scent, set off in pursuit of him who in breaching that most holy of promises to a lady had become a fugitive, and a criminal once more.

Hobbling along behind them all, shaking his fist and with his eyes flashing with just anger, was the High Judge, who cried, *"There will be no second chance!"*

All night long Toad cowered and shivered in the Wild Wood as the manhunt gradually closed in on him. What fearsome noises he heard in that dark dank place, what horrible eyes and faces within the roots of trees and what reaching crooked arms and claws within their ancient branches!

"O despair, I am done for now!" wept Toad.

Yet when the sun began to rise, Toad arose as well, and the dark fearsome shadows and noises of that place put fear in him no more. What he had seen of matrimony appeared to him to be more fearsome by far than incarceration in the Town Gaol, a trial, and a final and irrevocable sentence. In that was the greater liberty. He turned and made his way back to the Badger's house and there, with his friends watching sadly, he gave himself into the arms of the Law.

To only one present had he any word to say, and that was his young friend the Count.

"As these honest men are my witness," said Toad, pointing to the Senior Bishop, the Commissioner of Police and the High Judge, "I commend you to take a better road than I did. Be good, be kind to others, and think of yourself last of all!"

Then, these worthy sentiments well spoken, Toad was taken into custody, placed into a dark and shiny motorcar upon whose doors were painted the words "Town Constabulary". Then he was taken back to a place he had hoped never to see more – the remotest, most inhospitable dungeon in the Town Castle.

·XII·
Toad Triumphant

Toad's return to custody in the Town Castle was not much cheered by the familiar and doleful sight of the gaoler who had been in charge of him two years before.

"Welcome back, sir, I hope you have had a good holiday outside," he said.

"You go up those stairs," said one of the gaoler's young colleagues, feeling that the dazed and miserable Toad might need direction to Reception, where he must have his head shaved and don prison garb.

"It's all right," said Toad's friendly gaoler; "this one's a regular and knows the way."

"Will it go so hard with me?" asked Toad later, ensconced in his damp cell, with only a small, high barred window for light, and a few planks of wood for a bed.

"O, they'll hang you this time, sir, for certain, but in your case, since you're a gentleman, I'm sure they'll try to make a good swift job of it."

Toad wept.

"There, there, sir, don't be too unhappy. You've come in on a Sunday so there's two slices of bread and dripping for tea instead of just the one."

"When will my trial come up?"

"Tomorrow morning, first thing, Mr Toad. Yours is a special, I'm told, and they want to get it over and done with."

"Does it matter what I plead?"

"Not from where you sit, no sir, but it'll go hard with you if you plead guilty —"

"But I *am* guilty."

"Well, so you may be; most of us are. But the lawyers like to have something to argue about so they can earn their fees by proving what they already know. You'd be best to say —"

"I am guilty," said Toad obstinately, "and that's what I shall plead."

Toad's trial proved to be complex and involved, since the crimes included insult and injury, in person and in mind, to representatives of Justice, Law and the Established Church.

The fact that he did not deny his guilt regarding the

main charge of breach of promise, despite a good deal of pressure from his lawyer to counter with all kinds of nonsense involving alibis, false identity, unbalanced minds and extenuating circumstances, did not seem to change the course of the trial very much.

He sat once more in that uncomfortable chair wherein he had been tried on one hundred and sixteen charges two years previously, in the same court room, and before the same judges, the High Judge himself once more presiding.

Their wigs, their long faces, their convoluted language were bad enough, but the presence of the Commissioner of Police, representing the nation's constables, and the Senior Bishop, in his role as Prelate in Judgment of the Ecclesiastical Court-in-Sitting, could not but impress on all those present, the accused in particular, that this was a Final Court from which the harshest Findings and the most brutal Punishments would (quite properly) be due.

As generally expected, Toad was found guilty on each and every count, with sentencing to follow the next morning. It was early that morning, while he was waiting to be summoned for his final appearance in court, that he asked his gaoler for pen and paper, that he might write a letter.

He sat and thought a good deal before he wrote down what he wanted, tears coursing down his face and making a mess of the ink. But he finished it at last and summoned his gaoler again.

"Pray, can you do me a small service? Please see that this missive is sent to my friend Mr Badger of the Wild Wood."

"It'll have to be read by the Governor and censored as necessary," said the gaoler, "and the High Judge will have to read it too."

"I think there is nothing in it to which objection can be found," said Toad. "Now please take it to them right away, for I shall be called into court in less than an hour."

How right he was, for an hour later Toad was back in his cell, a condemned criminal. How long and full his life had been, yet how swiftly the High Judge had donned the black cap and pronounced sentence of death by hanging!

"Life's certainly upsetting, sir," observed his morose gaoler, "and does take sudden turns. Here today and gone tomorrow, eh, Mr Toad?"

The gaoler's laugh was like the tolling of a bell at evensong.

"Not tomorrow," said Toad; "the day after that. Did you send that letter?"

"Yes, Mr Toad, don't you worry about that."

The letter arrived at the Badger's house at the same time as news that a guilty verdict had been passed, and sentence of death by hanging pronounced upon the hapless Toad. For a time the letter was ignored, for though the sentence had been expected it was a shock when it was finally heard.

"I am sad that my return to the River Bank has been accompanied by such grievous goings-on," said Mr Brock, "and that my son's first experience of the River Bank finds us all in mourning. If there is any comfort to be had at all in this, it is that my father can at least look forward to good years ahead with Ratty and Mole safe and well, for that might have been a different story, might it not?"

They took a little comfort from this, but dead did the September sun seem, and muted the colours of autumn. Nor, when they read it, did Toad's letter offer them much cheer.

My dear friends,
    It has all gone against me and I shall not survive the week. I await final sentence this morning but none doubts the outcome. Therefore, lest I am in no state to write later, I do so now with two final requests.
    First, watch out for the Madame's son, for he is good at heart, and always did well by me. He will have need of friends such as yourselves if he is to avoid that road I have taken.
    Secondly, and even though you will call it empty vanity and false conceit, please me by inaugurating the statue of Roman triumph that the Madame completed in my image before my return, which was intended as a wedding gift. I prefer to be remembered so than as one tried by Society, condemned to execution, and swung from the gallows.
    Alas, they have denied me my last wish here, and all I am allowed for a cigar is a clay pipe of shag, and for champagne a pint of Policeman's Punch. In vain have I protested that shag and ale are not suited to Toad's style or taste. Therefore, when my statue is finally revealed, toast my health in my best champagne and smoke a Havana each in my memory. I shall be very much obliged.
    Farewell from your old friend,
        Toad of Toad Hall

"We must do Toad's bidding," said the Badger sombrely, "and honour and remember his good spirit and intentions for others as readily as we shall seek to forget his ignominious end."

"But is there nothing we can do for him, nothing at all?" said the Rat, who now regretted most bitterly his resolve in making Toad return to Toad Hall, despite the protestations of all his friends that in the end Toad's undoing was his own fault.

"We could not protect our old friend from himself forever," the Badger had said, "and I'm sure that Mole would say just the same. I have racked my brains for a way out but can find none. So too has Prendergast."

They turned to Toad's trusty and able servant and saw his sadness.

"I feel I have let my master down, gentlemen. And yet I take comfort in the discipline of my profession. You see, the Final Article of the Professional Butler's Code, which as you know I had a hand in wording, suggests that when a master is in *mortal* difficulty the well-trained butler, may I say the *professional* butler, will always be able to find a solution to his woes. Such a butler must strive for perfection in the art and science of his craft, and never give up.

"Therefore, gentlemen, sad though I am, I shall not give up till that moment when I hear, and on the best authority, of my master's demise. Till then, as the Senior Bishop is inclined to say of matters in general, and spiritual despair in particular, there is always hope and I shall continue to seek a solution."

"Well then," said the Badger, concluding this mournful discussion, "we shall cause Toad's statue to be erected on the morning, and at the hour, of his demise, which is to say in two days' time at midday. Till then do as Prendergast suggests, do not give up hope that a solution may be found.

"But before I depart I think this may be the appropriate moment to read to you the brief note I have had from Madame d'Albert-Chapelle, who has been unfairly vilified in this affair. It is to her credit that once her initial distress at being jilted was over she did what she could to rescind the action for breach of promise. But as I warned, whilst the wheels of Justice are slow to start, they have proved impossible to stop.

"She writes simply, *'Dear Monsieur Badger, I am very sad for my cousin Monsieur Toad, but I have not succeeded to get him liberty a second time. It is the guillotine for him. I shall always be unhappy for this, but remember with affection my stay with you at the River Bank. Commend me most especially to Mr Prendergast for his many kindnesses and give him this little drawing I made of him. With salutations, Madame d'Albert.'"*

The Badger handed the little sketch to Prendergast, in which she had depicted him in the pose of pouring tea.

"Thank you, sir, I shall treasure it always," said he, putting it in his pocket. "Now, if I may –"

Only then, for the first time, did Prendergast betray any emotion over his master's fate, and there was no one there who did not understand why he swiftly hurried away back to the Hall and his own private thoughts, for surely it is much against the Butler's Code to show one's tears.

Yet none there could have guessed that that was to be the last they saw of Prendergast, apart, that is, from the Otter who, up early the following morning, saw a very extraordinary sight emerging from the gates of Toad Hall. It was a horse at full gallop, and on its back was Prendergast, booted, behatted and rigged up for a long, hard journey, and the direction in which he turned the horse, before the Otter had a chance to hail him, was the Town.

The Otter felt it best to gather the Badger and the Rat, Nephew and Brock together to go to the Hall to investigate. All was in impeccable order, and various notices had been left in Prendergast's hand giving instructions for the maintenance of the Hall and even suggesting two possible and most worthy successors to himself: namely Mr Edwards of Fulham Palace, or Mr Waller of the Blenheim Estate.

"Ah," sighed the Rat, "the strain was too much for him after all."

But when the Otter ventured below-stairs to the butler's pantry, he found the only evidence of the butler's distress and haste. A half-drunk glass of sherry, an ink well with its top unclosed and its pen uncleaned of the ink used in writing his final instruction. The gaslight still burning –

"Most unlike Prendergast not to turn it off; he must have been very overwrought," murmured the Otter.

There seemed only one clear clue to the faithful butler's purpose and desperate intent. For the Code he followed so carefully was also there upon his writing bureau. Between its pages a piece of paper had been placed which, on examination, proved to be that little sketch which the Madame had sent him via the Badger the day before.

"But what possible effect can that have had upon so worthy a butler to push him into headlong flight?" said the Badger. Then he paused a moment, a look of surprise and dawning wonder upon his wise face, and he murmured, "Unless we do him a grave injustice –"

"Look!" said the Otter in alarm. "See which page this drawing marked."

They saw that it was at Article Five of the Code.

"Read it, Otter," said the Badger in a voice that suggested he might be beginning to understand now what was afoot.

"If the Master's life is threatened, it shall be the duty of a professional butler to offer his life first which, if accepted, shall be repaid with an honorarium of one week's holiday prior to said life's cessation –"

The Otter read no more, for the gist was all too plain.

"What does he intend to do?" said the Otter, aghast.

"Let us see what we can find in the rest of the Hall," said the Badger, calmer and more hopeful for Toad now than he had been for many weeks.

They explored the rooms, and it was Brock who found something else, this time in the conservatory. It was a champagne bucket, devoid of ice or a champagne bottle, but quite clearly ready to receive these special items of cheer and celebration, most carefully arranged upon a table adjacent to Toad's favourite wicker chaise longue. With it was a box of Havanas, and the means to light them.

For: Mr. Toad.
of Toad Hall

Propped up against the champagne bucket was a sealed envelope addressed thus: *For Mr Toad of Toad Hall. To be opened only by himself, upon the occasion of his welcome return home.*

The hand was indubitably Prendergast's own, and there was no further clue as to the contents of the envelope, or Prendergast's intentions. Alone among them the Badger was calm, and by now almost cheerful.

"Badger, will you kindly tell us what you think is going on, for I can see you think something!" said the Rat, speaking for them all.

"I will only say," observed the Badger, after a moment's reflection, "that I doubt very much, very much indeed, that there is a butler in all the land who combines common sense and resourcefulness with courage and self-sacrifice in so great and bold a way as the inestimable Prendergast. But if I am right about what he proposes to do to save his Master's life, and thus fulfil the obligation of his Code, the matter is too delicate, too critical, too uncertain in its outcome, for it to be wise that I say more now."

The day, the hour, the last minutes of the execution of Toad's just and lawful sentence had come, and he sat now no longer in his cell. How homely that seemed compared to the cold clean-painted room they had brought him to now, whose only furniture was a hard wooden stool, on which he found himself sitting manacled and chained.

Through a barred window he could see the gallows, and hanging from it a rope and noose. For company there was a clock upon the wall, whose minute hand stood at

three minutes before noon, and his gaoler, who sought even at this late hour to cheer Toad up.

"That's a new rope they've got in for you, sir, which is thoughtful, is it not, for it guards against breakages."

"I suppose it does," said Toad, upon whom an astonishing calm had descended. He had stared into the void of matrimony, and seen eternal horrors there, and despite all, the gallows seemed to him a swifter and more humane end.

"Then again," said his affable warder, "they've got in the Senior Bishop to say last prayers and rites, the Commissioner of Police, just to make sure you don't escape, and the High Judge himself, to see his sentence is properly executed, if you'll pardon the expression. It's a high honour to have all three watching over you to the last, Mr Toad."

"I'm glad of it," said Toad.

The clock clicked a minute more, which made one minute less and two to go. At which signal the three important personages the gaoler had mentioned appeared upon the gallows stand in the courtyard outside, and the warder took Toad's arm.

"I think it's time for a breath of fresh air, Mr Toad, if you follow my meaning. I hope you have found that I have been able to keep you cheerful to the last. You'll find that Albert the Executioner goes about his business in a very affable kind of way. He's more friendly than the last one they had, and very inclined to invite you round to meet the wife."

"I'm glad to hear it," said Toad.

Toad was led out into the open air and sunshine, up a

few steps towards a large gentleman, a good deal larger than anybody else, who was wearing a black hood. The executioner approached Toad and placed the noose about his neck.

"Didn't know this was one of yours, Frederick," said he to the gaoler, for they were old friends and had done this kind of work together more than once.

Then, turning to Toad, he said, "That's right, sir, stand just there, if you will, and I would be obliged if you did not move your feet. How's the wife, Frederick?"

"Keeping well, thank you, Albert."

With Toad well placed and nicely noosed the Senior Bishop said, "Mr Toad of Toad Hall, have you any final words?"

"Not on my own behalf, no, for I am glad to be finding a final liberty," said Toad, a craven coward no more, it seemed. "But I beg you, and you in particular, Your High Lordship, to take care of the Madame's son, for he means no harm and needs a little guidance now and then. I am past redemption, but he —"

Toad's last speech was interrupted by a rattling of the courtyard door, and a messenger came running.

"Message for His Lordship, if you please."

A note was handed to the High Judge who quickly read it, and then took the Commissioner of Police aside. Whatever he told him, it made that gentleman look very furious, and he blew a whistle and spoke to several constables, who went off about an urgent task. Then the High Judge spoke to the Senior Bishop, who went quite white and looked most horrified before falling upon his knees and offering up a silent prayer. Then he gathered up his purple skirts, called for his Chaplain and dashed off on urgent business.

The High Judge said, "Take the prisoner to his cell. Execution of sentence is postponed for twenty-four hours."

With that he too was gone.

"I really think," said Toad, considerably irritated, "that those gentlemen might have listened to my speech right to the end."

"Never mind," said his gaoler, leading him away; "you'll have a chance to finish it tomorrow."

But within twenty-four hours Toad was at liberty once more, and on his way home, astonished, bemused, and for once not singing his own praises but those of another.

When the High Judge had first read that missive that reached him a few moments before the execution of the sentence upon Mr Toad he was very much astonished, yet not entirely unhappy to have an excuse to postpone matters for a day or two.

It was true that he was known as a hanging judge, but it was also true that he was one of those who did not rest easy unless he felt he was satisfied that the punishment he decreed truly fitted the crime. To his mind, hanging often did, and so he had little compunction sending those who came before him into that final cul de sac.

Once in a while, however, there came before him one in whom he saw the possibilities of redemption, and for whom, reprehensible though their crimes were – and Mr Toad's were singularly bad, particularly his offences in the field of botany – he felt a less conventional punishment might be suitable. But though he had racked his brains he

could not seem to find anything better than hanging for
Mr Toad, and had therefore donned the black cap and
passed that ultimate sentence.

Then came the letter, and suddenly all seemed
changed. Mr Toad's crimes – and the punishment thereof
– were cast in a very different complexion indeed.

Indeed, so surprised was the High Judge by what the
missive contained that he read it several times, as well as
the clipping from the Town's evening newspaper that was
attached to it.

"*Your comments would be welcome,*" the editor of that
organ wrote briefly to him. The clipping was headlined
with words that said it all: "HIGH JUDGE'S FORMER
BUTLER ELOPES WITH JILTED FRENCH BRIDE."

Then, in type less bold, "*Love-nest found in Harwich.
They take the packet to Australia tomorrow.*"

Then in type even less bold, "*Mystery of why lady's 'best
man', the 'Hang-'em-High' High Judge, was allowed to pass
judgment on her former fiancé.*"

Then, in ordinary-sized type, the sorry tale itself,
which told of how the butler Prendergast, a Lothario of
the worst kind it seemed, had plotted with Madame
d'Albert–Chapelle, infamous jilted bride in the case of
Mr Toad, to elope on the very morning of his execution.

"*Even as that generous and courageous sporting gentleman
puts his neck in the hangman's noose, the Cunning Countess
and the Brutal Butler will be heartlessly watching the coast of
our once-just land recede as their boat sets sail for pastures new.
Rarely in our legal history –*" and so the story continued,
lurid detail after lurid detail.

The High Judge was very well used to the rantings of

the popular press, but he was shaken to the core by these events, if they were true.

The Madame marrying a *butler*, that was the gist of it, the beginning and the end of it. He saw it now almost too late, as once before he had been slow to see the nobility and courage that Mr Toad hid under his unpre-possessing and criminal-seeming exterior.

"He must have known, or guessed, of her dalliance with Prendergast only at that very last moment when, too much of a gentleman to declare his suspicions, he fled," the High Judge told himself. "He is a better judge of the ladies than myself, no doubt, but even he had been taken in by her French charm, and by the seeming pro-bity of Prendergast.

"A countess and a butler! We really cannot, and will not, hang a gentlemen for breach of promise to such a lady as that!"

The wheels of justice, the Badger had observed, run slowly at first, but then when they turn more swiftly they cannot be easily stopped. Not, that is, unless scandal and exposure in high places is involved; not unless those in high places need it to be so; not unless at one fell swoop the might of the Law, the equity of Justice and the wisdom of the Established Church might seem to be undermined, and fairly so, in the gutter and quality press alike.

Then the wheels of justice can indeed be stopped, and put very rapidly in reverse.

Yet, mused the High Judge, when appropriate instruc-tions had been given to this effect, and counter-signed and sealed by the Senior Bishop and Commissioner of

Police, and Toad pardoned, yet – and he could not but think that shocking though the elopement was, perhaps he had underestimated Mr Prendergast. Could it be that eloping with the Countess was the only way left open to him to get his master off the hook?

"Hmmm," mused the High Judge, and finally he smiled, and admitted that, given all he knew of Prendergast, it might indeed be so.

"So then, what shall we do with Mr Toad, for he certainly has done *some* wrong?"

Just then there was a knock at his door and his clerk announced a visitor, a very young visitor, a Count.

"Aha!" said the High Judge in a voice of expectation.

"I 'ave been sent by Monsieur Prendergast," began the youth, who looked tired and rather miserable, "who is now my new papa."

"They are already wed?"

"Oui, monsieur, this morning, by the *capitaine* of the ship in which they have sailed at the hour when Monsieur Toad was guillotined."

"Hanged," corrected the High Judge; "but he is still alive."

"Formidable!" said the Count, a look of relief upon his face.

"He will be pardoned," said the High Judge.

"I 'ave a letter from Monsieur Prendergast," said the youth, handing over a letter in a hand the High Judge knew of old.

Your High Lordship
I hope you will forgive me for presuming upon our very long professional relationship, in the course of which you were kind

enough to suggest that if ever there was anything you might do for me then if it was in your power you would do it. You have been a kind and generous employer and always recompensed me fairly for my work, and it is a matter of pride that I have never taken up your offer.

I fancy, however, that my elopement with the Madame may change the complexion of things somewhat – indeed I trust it will, for Mr Toad is a good man at heart – though I must leave all that to chance and the popular newspapers. It is about the Madame's son I write now, and the thorny problem of a fitting punishment for Mr Toad, in the eventuality that his capital punishment will be set aside –

There was a good deal more in this vein, till finally Prendergast made the suggestion – that bold and most resourceful suggestion – that revealed to His Lordship the best way to proceed.

He read the letter again and looked up at last at the nervous youth.

"You did not wish to sail to Australia with your mother, then?"

"No, monsieur," he replied quietly.

"You wished, perhaps, to return to relatives in France?"

"Non, monsieur; I 'ave none I like," said he more quietly still.

"You have perhaps sufficient means to take an establishment of your own and − ?"

"I 'ave money, monsieur, but I do not wish to live alone. Monsieur Prendergast 'as said you would know what I should do."

"Did he now?" said the High Judge, the glimmer of a smile upon his face.

"'E said 'e was certain of it!"

"Humph!" said the High Judge. "Well then −" and he stared at the Madame's son for a long, long time.

Finally he said, "I shall ask you a question and upon your reply very much will depend concerning your future, and another's. Tell me, but think very carefully before you do, what has been the happiest and the most contented time of your life?"

The youth seemed surprised and fell silent, thinking perhaps of the many presents he had been given throughout his life, the exotic places taken, the treats received and the indulgences given. The High Judge saw a great many fleeting memories pass across his face, but he saw no sign of happiness, and none of remembered contentment.

But then, like a sun beginning to shine at last, a look

of happiness came to his face, and memory of a time of past contentment.

"Well?" said the High Judge.

"It was an afternoon and 'e —"

"Who?" asked the High Judge gently.

"Monsieur Toad, he took me fishing but —"

"Yes? Take your time, there is plenty of it."

"But it was not that, monsieur, that made me 'appy, it was how 'e showed me about the line, and the trace, and which fly was best and —"

"Mmm?"

"It was when Monsieur Toad showed me 'ow to tie a hook. That was the best time. I was content. Then, monsieur, we —"

And the High Judge listened to an account of the afternoon and evening Toad and his young ward shared after their departure from the farmer's wife and daughter, a time of fishing, of a memorable feast, and of a river gliding by.

"How would you like," said the High Judge when the tale was done, "to go and live with Mr Toad? Do you think he would look after you?"

The youth thought some more and said finally, with a smile, "I think that 'e would try, monsieur, try very 'ard."

"Yes," said His Lordship, "I do believe he would."

There were instructions to give then and documents to prepare, which contained a great many words and phrases such as "Custody" and "Ward of the High Court" and "In honour bound" and many more besides.

Then Toad was summoned and told his fate, which was in the High Judge's view one harder by far than hanging, for the youth would make many demands, and they would increase as the years went by, so much so that they would try the patience of a saint. And all agreed that Mr Toad of Toad Hall would have to work very hard if he was to become one of those.

So it was that the admirable Prendergast laid down his life for Toad, and by turning an honourable jilted noble-lady into a dishonourable French elopee, whose passions led her to the butler's pantry door and beyond it, saved his master's skin. And, it must be said, provided Prendergast with a bride whose happiness was matched only by his own; and her son with a Toad in loco paren-tis who might in time learn to do for another what he could never quite do for himself.

So it was quite natural for Toad to be singing the praises of Prendergast all the way from the Town to Toad Hall, and getting the young ward of court, who was now duly assigned into his care, to sing them too.

But old habits die hard, if they ever die at all, and Toad could not but reflect that if he had thought of it earlier he would have prepared a speech.

Then, as the motor-car turned through his own gates once more and Toad saw his friends ready and waiting for him, to give him welcome, and perhaps praise and per-haps tell him what a clever animal he was, several possi-bilities for a speech occurred, for there was very much that he might say.

Even as they shook his hand, and that of his young ward, Toad had begun the preliminaries to speechifying and strutting about.

"There's to be a ceremony, is there? We're to inaugurate the statue, are we? Right away, I trust! Right now, in fact!"

While in the shadows, now to one side of the Badger, now by himself and then behind the Mole and then again by himself, Toad's ward wandered, uneasy with himself, not quite sure what he must do.

So much noise, so many people, and all so pleased to see Monsieur Toad.

Out onto the terrace they went, and from there to stand before Toad's new statue so recently erected and now ready to inaugurate.

The Madame had done her work boldly and well, and future generations gazing upon the statue she had made might form a very different, and more favourable, impression of Toad of Toad Hall than those who knew him in life.

For his bronze persona stood upon its pedestal as proud and triumphant as any victorious Caesar. He wore the flowing robes of a Roman ruler, and upon his feet were leather sandals that spoke of a freer and warmer climate than was customary for the River Bank. Upon his head (and, indeed, intertwined with rather more hair than the real Toad sported) was a wreath of laurel, while one hand held aloft the rod of state and supreme authority. So taken had she been by her subject, Toad, that she had discarded altogether any rendering of the Mole, the Badger and the Rat as humble legates, or in any other role – no doubt to their considerable relief.

It was upon the expression of the face that the Madame had bestowed her very greatest genius, for its look of triumphant self-satisfaction combined Augustan majesty with Claudian cunning, and the military might of a Julius Caesar with the very slightest hint of the indulgence and profligacy of Nero.

The general direction of its gaze was skyward, perhaps even heavenward, and certainly a good deal beyond bothering to read the Latin inscription which remained inscribed upon the statue's pedestal, which the Badger had obligingly rendered into English for the satisfaction of the Mole's curiosity: "Humility above all".

The Badger opened that special bottle of wine the Mole had made; the Rat and the Otter, with Brock's help, gathered some chairs and a table or two that they might sit down once the speeches were over, and talk as so often in the past; Nephew and Grandson, already good friends, repaired to the kitchen to gather together whatever picnic they could find; Toad closed his eyes and mouthed and gestured a few grand phrases, taking the new statue and the theme of triumph for his inspiration; while his young ward stood all alone, not knowing what to do.

"Monsieur —"

"Not now, old chap, I've a speech to prepare."

"Monsieur, on the way here you promised that —"

"O yes, not today though; no time, you see, and all these fellows to entertain."

"Monsieur, but when might we — ?"

"There, everything's ready now. Why don't you sit down over there and join in the fun?"

The poor youth sat, and tried.

"Gentlemen and friends," began Toad, when he had

established some semblance of order and their glasses were charged, "there are a good many things —"

Toad's ward sat alone, and his gaze wandered towards the River.

"Gentlemen, I want to say, by which I mean I wish and intend to say —" Toad had wanted to say how glorious his return seemed to be, how triumphal, not at all unlike the return of an imperial emperor to Rome, no, not at all — but he stopped again, for his heart was not in it.

Meanwhile the Madame's son watched where the River flowed at the edge of the slope below them, majestic and slow, the light of the afternoon on its surface, and the colours of the autumn.

"Gentlemen, and friends," said Toad yet again, "I am glad to be back, but I — I am a little tired and so will leave the speeches to Mole and Ratty. Yes, gentlemen, to you both, for yours has been a great expedition and journey. But pray forgive me if I slip away for a time —"

"Toad, we want to hear you speak!" cried the Rat.

"You will do it a great deal better than we ever can," said the Mole.

But Toad would have none of it, none of it at all, and instead put down his glass and, as the others began to laugh and talk amongst themselves, he went over to where his ward sat alone.

"There, that didn't take too long."

"Monsieur?" said the youth, perking up a little.

"Didn't I promise to take you fishing?"

"Yes, monsieur —"

"Call me Toad, everybody else does. And didn't I promise to give you a rather particular fishing rod?"

"Ah, oui, monsieur – yes you did."

"Mind you, it is rather old now, and got a little charred in the great fire we had here a year or two ago, but it was amongst the few things I saved and I treasure it. It is the first rod I was given, and it is good for a beginner. You shall have it now."

Without further ado, Toad took the boy into the Hall and gave him a gift that money could not buy.

"When can we use it, Toad?" he asked, gaining in confidence all the while.

"Now!" said Toad carelessly, taking up another rod, and enough tackle for them both, and leading his young friend to a side door so that they did not get diverted by the others. "Straight away, in fact. There's no time like the present. That's always been my motto and it will do very well for you too, I dare say."

"No time like the present," repeated the happy youth.

"That's right," said Toad, and with rods and tackle in hand, they headed off together, towards the River Bank.

THE END

Publisher's Note

Readers who have enjoyed *Toad Triumphant* and would like to be informed about the author's future work should write to William Horwood at P.O. Box 446, Oxford, OX1 2SS.